Une Saison en Enfer
Les Illuminations

A Season in Hell
The Illuminations

ARTHUR

Une Saison en Enfer
Les Illuminations

A NEW TRANSLATION BY

New York OXFORD UNIVERSITY

RIMBAUD

A Season in Hell
The Illuminations

ENID RHODES PESCHEL

PRESS London Oxford

Acknowledgments

For their careful reading of the manuscript of this book and the many valuable suggestions they offered, I wish to express my great indebtedness to Professors Henri Peyre, Reinhard Kuhn, William Berg, K. F. Schofer, Albert Sonnenfeld and R. Etiemble. I am grateful also to Stephanie Golden of Oxford for the many perceptive recommendations she made after a meticulous study of my manuscript. And, finally, it is a pleasure to thank my editor, John W. Wright, for his enthusiasm, which supported me throughout the preparation of this work for publication.

A number of my translations of Rimbaud's poetry were first published in somewhat different form in the following places:

"Nocturne vulgaire," *Prairie Schooner*, Vol. 42, No. 3 (Fall 1968); "Vies III," *Laurel Review*, Vol. 10, No. 2 (Fall 1970); "Les Ponts," *Discourse*, Vol. 13, No. 1 (Winter 1970); "Après le déluge," *Dragonfly* (1970); "Veillées," *Poet Lore*, Vol. 64, No. 4 (Winter 1969); "Being Beauteous," *Orion* (May–June 1971); "Guerre," "Ornières," *Scimitar and Song*, Vol. 31, No. 3 (June–July 1969); "Jeunesse I: Dimanche," *Bachaet*, Vol. II, No. 1 (June 1970); "Honte," *Pembroke Alumna*, Vol. 43, No. 4 (October 1968); "Jeunesse IV," *Best in Poetry* (1970); "Mystique," *Essence*, No. 40 (Winter 1969–70); "Démocratie," *The Hobbit*, Vol. 1, No. 2 (1968); "A Une Raison," "Aube," "Métropolitain," *Contact* (1967); "Ville," "Angoisse," *Encounter* (1968); and "Vies I," *The New Renaissance*, Vol. I, No. 4 (1970).

OXFORD UNIVERSITY PRESS

London   Oxford   New York
Glasgow   Toronto   Melbourne   Wellington
Cape Town   Ibadan   Nairobi   Dar es Salaam   Lusaka   Addis Ababa
Delhi   Bombay   Calcutta   Madras   Karachi   Lahore   Dacca
Kuala Lumpur   Singapore   Hong Kong   Tokyo

Foreword

Enid Rhodes Peschel is a fine young poet. Her verse, which has appeared in many magazines, is refreshingly free from all mannerism and from the childish affectation of violence and brutality which will soon date many poets of the nineteen-sixties. It is unashamedly romantic, in the sense that it does not repudiate sensuous delight, richness of imagery, harmony and sentiment. Her good fortune is that, while fully at home in the literature of the English language, she has made an especial study of the poetry of France. She wrote a Ph.D. thesis at Harvard under the direction of one of the best Rimbaud scholars of our time, Wilbur M. Frohock. She teaches at Yale, where her courses on Baudelaire and on Rimbaud have attracted many of the young rebels; for, appearances notwithstanding, never perhaps has the youth of America been more athirst for poetry in all its forms (in music and painting and fiction, and in its fight for a clean environment and for the poetry of peace and justice) than it is today. Rimbaud and Nietzsche are two of the geniuses to whom, in its half-conscious or only half-confessed search for heroes, the young people of several continents have turned, in disgust with their own age, in the seventh decade of our century.

A critic who is also a poet was ideally fit to undertake the difficult task of rendering into English the poetry of Rimbaud. Other poets and scholars had already risen to the challenge: Delmore Schwartz, Louise Varèse and Wallace Fowlie, among them. The mysterious beauty of Rimbaud's texts, their formidable energy, the directness with which they assault the reader and compel him to submit to the poet's sway should indeed tempt new translators in every generation. Like all very great works, *A Season in Hell* and the *Illuminations* are to be reinterpreted and relived every ten years.

The translation here offered is faithful, precise, literal, yet never prosaic or ponderous. It does not, and it should not, paraphrase,

or weaken the force of the original. It does not make clear what is elliptic and ambiguous. It may not altogether replace the text for those who cannot decipher it. For those who have even a slight acquaintance with French, the English version will be a help and a source of enhanced emotion. Rimbaud was the first writer (then Mallarmé and, since then, many moderns) by whom language was no longer used to transmit a preëxisting meaning to express and convey a feeling or an idea. It became a sacred value, a set of *carmina,* or magical spells, aiming at "changing life," as Rimbaud puts it, at creating what did not yet exist. The poet saw himself as a Promethean ravisher of fire, or even as God himself uttering his Creator's fiat.

Contrary moods are juxtaposed by the poet. His vertiginous mind welcomes opposite thoughts or resolutions. He now curses life, now accepts it resignedly. Desperately, he attempts to free himself from the fear of hell, instilled in him by his religious training. He longs to go back to the primitive, barbaric condition of a pagan, "a black"; at the same time, he realizes how vain is that nostalgia and wants to transcend all that is mediocre in his Christian, Western civilization. "One must be absolutely modern": shake women free from their slavery and reinvent love thereby, spurn the worn-out literary devices, transcend Christianity through more charity and through acceptance of the body as well as of the soul as vessels of the new truth.

There are a few spirits bold enough to contend that beautiful poetry should simply strike us with its full impetus, lure us to read it over and over, and that it stands in no need of commentary. Fortunate are those few. For the majority of us, however, literature—even more than a statue, a painting or a song—because it is rich with an underlying content of thought, of feeling, of self-analysis by the author, gains from being elucidated. Criticism should not aim at doing away with mystery, but at enabling the reader to perceive it with an even keener intensity than he would if unaided by commentaries. Enid Rhodes Peschel has added a penetrating and discreet introduction to her translation.

Ardent and, in truth, inconclusive and perhaps vain contro-
versies raged some years ago in France around the exact date at
which Rimbaud gave up poetry and turned his back on the Promethean ambitions of his seventeenth year. It may well be, indeed,
that the farewell which closes *A Season in Hell* may have been
only a tentative one and that Rimbaud composed, or copied from
earlier manuscripts, some of his *Illuminations* after the completion
of his lyrical and epic autobiography. The explosive beauty of those
evocations of cities, of unearthly landscapes, of vertiginous ascents
into the abode of angels, the forcefulness with which an adolescent
poet merges the sky, the sea and the land into a novel universe
which his genius conjures up and re-creates, make those *Illuminations* uniquely enigmatic and difficult to interpret or to render into
another language. Enid Rhodes Peschel has been served by her
poet's power over words in her own language and by her scrupulous
fidelity to the original. Her rendering of these mysterious texts,
free from any obtrusive comments, dense and swift, has the supreme merit of a translation: it lures the reader back to a more
intense enjoyment of the original.

Rimbaud is, along with Victor Hugo, the most imaginative of
French poets. An idea for him at once becomes an image—con-
ceptual thinking takes place only in imaginative terms. A writer
less scrupulously faithful to the text than Enid Peschel might con-
strain that "rapturous and explosive destructivism of Rimbaud"
(Hart Crane's phrase in a letter of June 20, 1926 to Waldo Frank).
This study and this translation of the most significant single long
poem in French literature and of the *Illuminations* constitute an
achievement felicitously blending the gifts of a scholar with those
of a poet.

Henri M. Peyre
Sterling Professor Emeritus
Yale University

Distinguished Professor
Graduate Center
City University of New York

For my mother
my first teacher of poetry
in literature and in life

Contents

Une Saison en Enfer
Les Illuminations

A Season in Hell
The Illuminations

Rimbaud's Life and Work

I! I who called myself a seer or an angel, exempt from all morality, I am restored to the earth, with a duty to seek, and rugged reality to embrace! Peasant!

Farewell

Born on October 20, 1854, Jean-Nicolas-Arthur Rimbaud grew up in Charleville (Ardennes), a town in northeastern France near the Belgian border. His father, Frédéric Rimbaud, an officer who had risen through the ranks of the French army, abandoned the family when Arthur, the second of five children, was six years old. The poet's mother, née Vitalie Cuif, a parvenu peasant, was stubborn, narrow-minded and fanatically religious.

In 1870 a young teacher who wrote poetry, Georges Izambard, arrived at Arthur's school, the Collège de Charleville. Izambard encouraged Rimbaud and lent him books by Villon, Rabelais, Hugo and the Parnassian poets. While his teacher's guidance inspired Arthur, it did not always please his mother, who complained irately in a letter to Izambard that he had lent her son a "dangerous book," Victor Hugo's *Les Misérables*.

The same year, 1870, during which Rimbaud composed twenty-two poems, signaled the awakening of his genius. Writing about the joys of nature, dreams, freedom, pagan eroticism and rebellion against Christianity, the young author sent three poems: *Feeling* (*Sensation*), *Sun and Flesh* (*Soleil et chair*) and *Ophelia*

Arthur Rimbaud (seated) and his brother, Frédéric, as communicants (1866). (French Cultural Services, New York)

(*Ophélie*) to Théodore de Banville because he hoped that the Parnassian poet would publish them in the second edition of *Contemporary Parnassus* (*Le Parnasse contemporain*). Rimbaud's verses arrived too late, however; the review was already complete.

Another poem composed that year was *The Sleeper of the Valley* (*Le Dormeur du val*), a reaction to death and the Franco-Prussian War. Up to the last line the "young soldier" of the poem seems to be dreaming on the grass, but the sonnet's delicate sensuousness is shattered by the ironic realization that there are "two red holes" in the sleeper's right side.

During the Franco-Prussian War schools closed, Izambard left Charleville, and Rimbaud dreamed of leaving home. In August 1870 he wrote *At the Concert* (*A la musique*), satirizing Charleville, its bourgeois inhabitants and the military band's weekly concerts held in the "railroad square."

One day that August Rimbaud suddenly boarded a train for Paris. Since the fifteen-year-old boy did not have enough money to pay for his ride, he was thrown into Mazas prison when he reached the French capital. A week later he finally wrote to Izambard, explaining what he had done. Izambard rescued him from jail and ultimately returned him to his mother. But Arthur did not remain long in Charleville.

By the end of the next month, he ran away again; this time he spent two weeks walking — from Charleville to Belgium and then to Izambard's home in Douai, in the north of France. He arrived there half-starved, his clothes in tatters. *My Bohemia* (*Ma Bohème*) describes the poet's happy feelings of intoxicating liberation as he wandered in his ragged apparel during those "good September evenings" when dewdrops seemed to him "like a wine of strength." After this second escapade Rimbaud was delivered to his home by the police.

In Charleville he felt bored, frustrated, repressed. From there, on November 2, 1870, he wrote to Izambard: "I am dying, I am decomposing in the dullness, in the nastiness, in the grayness. . . .

Rimbaud in October 1871.
(French Cultural Services, New York)

Lithograph of Rimbaud by Picasso.
(Collection H. Matarasso)

I ought to set out again, today even." It is not surprising then that five months later, when the Collège de Charleville reopened as the war was drawing to a close, the sixteen-year-old poet refused to return to the classroom. He had new ideas and projects.

THE "LETTRE DU VOYANT"

On May 15, 1871, Rimbaud wrote to his friend Paul Demeny the document now celebrated as the "Lettre du voyant," in which he described his revolutionary theories about poetry and life. Denouncing, debasing and dismissing almost every poet preceding him for two thousand years, Rimbaud leaps from thought to thought and from idea to image, in a manifesto as arrogant as it is sobering.

The author is clearly aware of the perils inherent in the poetic enterprise he is prescribing for himself.

What he wants is something *"new, — ideas and forms,"* Rimbaud declares. To accomplish his goal, he says that he will make himself a *voyant*.[1] What is a *voyant*? For Rimbaud, the *voyant* is not only a poet-prophet-visionary, but a poet who practices the "long, immense and reasoned *deranging* of *all his senses*" in order to reach a transcendent state, which he calls the "unknown." His use of the word "reasoned" implies that his sensuous disordering is both intentional and systematic; his plan is not at all haphazard, and he insists upon the fact that it is a poet who is acting:

> The first study for the man who wishes to be a poet is his own self-knowledge, entire; he seeks his soul, he inspects it, he tempts it, apprehends it. As soon as he knows it, he must cultivate it! That seems simple. . . . — But it is a matter of making the soul monstrous: in the fashion of the *compra-chicos*,[2] so! Imagine a man implanting and cultivating warts on his face.
>
> I say that it is necessary to be a *voyant*, to make oneself a *voyant*.
>
> The Poet makes himself a *voyant* through a long, immense and reasoned *deranging* of *all his senses*. All the forms of love, of suffering, of madness; he tries to find himself, he exhausts in himself all the poisons, to keep only their quintessences. Unutterable torture in which he needs all his faith, all his superhuman strength, in which he becomes among all men the great invalid, the great criminal, the great accursed one, — and the supreme Savant! — For he arrives at the *unknown!* Since he has cultivated his soul, already rich, more than any-one else! He arrives at the unknown, and although, crazed, he would end up by losing the understanding of his visions,

1. I use the French word *voyant* because there is no exact equivalent in English. All translations of quoted material are my own.

2. The *comprachicos* in Victor Hugo's *L'Homme qui rit* (1869) are kid-nappers who mutilate children in order to exhibit them as monsters.

he has seen them! Let him die in his leaping through unheard-of and unnameable things: other horrible workers will
come; they will begin on the horizons where the other col-
lapsed!

Rimbaud's expressed desire in this letter to experience "all the
forms of love" helps explain his liaison with Paul Verlaine; his
craving to exhaust in himself "all the poisons, to keep only their
quintessences," sheds light on his use of alcohol, hashish and other
intoxicants.

But these words of ecstatic prophecy also foretell the *voyant*'s
defeat. When he reaches his goal, when he becomes the "supreme
Savant," Rimbaud says, he will become "crazed" and lose the under-
standing of his visions. Here he does not seem to mind the prospect
of the *voyant*'s death: "Let him die," he declares with bravado.
Still, these words leave an ominous impression: in the *voyant*'s
rapture lies his ruination. *The Drunken Boat* (*Le Bateau ivre*),
composed several months later, repeats the poetic pattern sketched
here: rebellion and sensuous derangement lead to ecstasy and
destruction.

It is impossible not to note the theatrical nature of the letter
itself: the poet postures, assigns roles to himself, provides an inter-
mission and "songs." Even his description of how he becomes a
voyant is dramatic:

> For *I* is another person. If brass awakes as a bugle, it is not
> at all its fault. This is plain to me: I am a witness to the birth
> of my thought: I look at it, I listen to it: I draw a stroke of
> the bow: the symphony makes its stir in the depths, or comes
> with a leap upon the stage.

Here, the first person subject is suddenly annexed to a third person
verb: a persona's separation from one part of the author is vividly
proclaimed. Dialoguing with his other roles (of which there are
many), criticizing their flights of fantasy, the voice of reality, the
brutal and ironic "I," will generate much of the dramatic tension

in Rimbaud's poetry. This tension creates a twofold vision, permitting both an internal and an external, a subjective and an objective view of Rimbaud's self-characterizations. Yet this "I" is ultimately destructive, for in ridiculing the author's other selves, this bitter voice probably prepared the way for Rimbaud's renunciation of poetry.

The *voyant*, Rimbaud claims, will find a new and liberating language of perfect and total comprehension: "This language will be of the soul for the soul, epitomizing everything, scents, sounds, colors, thought seizing thought and reaching forth." Through his new language, the *voyant* "would be truly *a multiplier of progress!*" Rimbaud exclaims. "Poetry will no longer suit action to a rhythm; it *will be in the vanguard.*" Another Prometheus, the *voyant*-"thief of fire" will re-create something like the idealized state of "harmonious Life" that Rimbaud believed once existed in ancient Greece. He will liberate men, animals, language and poetic form: "if what he brings back from *over there* has form, he renders form; if it is formless, he renders the formlessness." Even women will be freed, Rimbaud proclaims:

> When the endless servitude of woman will be overthrown, when she will live for herself and by herself, man, — hitherto abominable, — having given her her release, she will be a poet, she also! Woman will discover some of the unknown! Will her worlds of ideas differ from ours? — She will discover strange, unfathomable, repellent, delicious things; we shall take them, we shall comprehend them.

At the end of the "Lettre du voyant" Rimbaud judges his immediate predecessors. In Alphonse de Lamartine, Victor Hugo, Théophile Gautier, Leconte de Lisle and Théodore de Banville he finds a few admirable qualities. Baudelaire, he claims, "is the first *voyant*, king of the poets, *a true God*"; however, Rimbaud criticizes Baudelaire's poetic form and the "overly artistic milieu" in which he lived. The "new school, called Parnassian, has two *voyants*,

Rimbaud in 1871. Sketch by his friend Ernest Delahaye. (French Cultural Services, New York)

Albert Mérat [3] and Paul Verlaine," Rimbaud adds. When Rimbaud wrote the "Lettre du voyant," Verlaine was already the author of *Saturnian Poems* (*Poèmes saturniens*, 1866) and *Gallant Festivals* (*Fêtes galantes*, 1869); his poems were also published in *Le Parnasse contemporain.*

VERLAINE

Four months after composing his literary manifesto, Rimbaud actually wrote to Verlaine. To the sixteeen-year-old's appeal for help — "I have formed the project of making a great poem, and I cannot work in Charleville. I am prevented from coming to Paris, being without resources" — Verlaine answered: "Come, dear great soul, one calls you, one waits for you." And so Rimbaud went to Paris.

3. Albert Mérat (1840–1909) is the author of *The Idol* (*L'Idole*, 1869), a sonnet collection in which each poem is devoted to a different part of the female body.

Coin de Table (*Corner of the Table*, 1872). Painting by Fantin-Latour. Seated (from left to right): P. Verlaine, A. Rimbaud, L. Valade, E. d'Hervilly and C. Pelletan; standing (from left to right): E. Bonnier, E. Blémont and J. Aicard. (Musée du Louvre; photo Bulloz)

Verlaine, then twenty-six, was married to the seventeen-year-old Mathilde Mauté de Fleurville. They lived in Montmartre with the girl's parents. At first Rimbaud was invited to stay with them, but his offensive behavior soon shocked Mathilde and her parents. Shortly after October 30, 1871, when Verlaine's son was born, Rimbaud fled from the abode on Rue Nicolet. Verlaine followed him, and the two men became lovers.

The older poet introduced Rimbaud to the literati of Paris, including Théodore de Banville, José-Maria de Hérédia, François Coppée, Charles Cros and Albert Mérat. Rimbaud's outrageous actions and language scandalized the Parnassian poets, however. In

Rimbaud in Paris (1872). Drawing by Paul Verlaine.
(French Cultural Services, New York)

July 1872 Rimbaud and Verlaine left France for Belgium and England.

During their tempestuous two-year liaison and within a year or two after it, Rimbaud wrote most of his finest poetry, including his *Derniers Vers*, *A Season in Hell* and the *Illuminations*. The *Derniers Vers* of the spring and summer of 1872 are his last poems that adhere (generally) to the traditional exigencies of rhyme and meter. *Shame (Honte)* is one of the most remarkable of these. My translation accompanies the French text:

HONTE	SHAME
Tant que la lame n'aura Pas coupé cette cervelle, Ce paquet blanc, vert et gras, A vapeur jamais nouvelle,	Not till the blade has cut clear through This brain, this mass of pale Fat matter, greenish-white in hue, Its exhalations stale,
(Ah! Lui, devrait couper son Nez, sa lèvre, ses oreilles, Son ventre! et faire abandon De ses jambes! ô merveille!)	(Ah! He should slit his nose, his lips, His ears, his paunch so full! Forsake his useless legs and hips! O what a miracle!)
Mais, non; vrai, je crois que tant Que pour sa tête la lame, Que les cailloux pour son flanc, Que pour ses boyaux la flamme,	Why, no; not till his aching brain Has felt the knife; his side, The jagged stones; his gut, the pain Of mounting flame inside:
N'auront pas agi, l'enfant Gêneur, la si sotte bête, Ne doit cesser un instant De ruser et d'être traître,	Until that time the trying child In brute stupidity Must not an instant cease his wild Deceit and treachery,

Comme un chat des Monts-
   Rocheux,
D'empuantir toutes sphères!
Qu'à sa mort pourtant, ô mon
   Dieu!
S'élève quelque prière!
	A Rocky Mountain cat, whose
	   breath
	Befouls all earth and air!
	And yet, O God, upon his death
	Let there arise some prayer!

In *Deliriums II* of *A Season in Hell* Rimbaud rewrote and used some of his lyrical poems of 1872.

On July 10, 1873, in Brussels, Verlaine, drunk and furious that Rimbaud was threatening to leave him, shot his young lover in the wrist. While Verlaine went to prison, Rimbaud returned to his mother's farm in Roche, where he completed *A Season in Hell*, an undertaking he had begun in the spring with a projected title "Pagan Book, or Negro Book." *Deliriums I* of this great work is clearly a poetic transposition of Rimbaud's life with Verlaine.

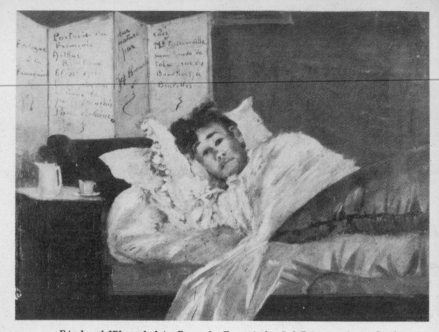

Rimbaud Wounded in Brussels. Portrait by Jef Rosman (ca. 1873).
The words on the screen read: "Epilogue in the French fashion.
Portrait of the Frenchman Arthur Rimbaud, wounded after drinking
by his intimate friend, the French poet Paul Verlaine. From life by
Jef Rosman. At the home of Madame Pincemaille, tobacconist, rue
des Bouchers, in Brussels." (French Cultural Services, New York)

Rimbaud was eighteen when he finished *A Season in Hell*; when
he was nineteen or twenty he stopped writing poetry. In 1874 he
returned to London, this time with the poet Germain Nouveau.
There Rimbaud recopied several of the *Illuminations*; perhaps he
even wrote some of them that year.

The problem of dating these enchanting and often hallucinatory
poems has never been completely resolved. The *Illuminations* were
first published in 1886 without Rimbaud's knowledge, since he had

already abandoned poetry and was living in Africa. Verlaine claimed that the *Illuminations* were written between 1873 and 1875; that is, they were probably created after Rimbaud finished *A Season in Hell*. Ernest Delahaye, however, said that the poems were composed between 1872 and 1873. By a study of Rimbaud's handwriting, H. de Bouillane de Lacoste tried to date the *Illuminations*[4] (he sees them as subsequent to *A Season in Hell*), but his conclusions are not completely convincing since he examined only a few copies of Rimbaud's handwriting; furthermore, the poems Lacoste studied may have been copies Rimbaud made long after he had written the original work.

No one really knows why or exactly when Rimbaud stopped writing poetry. In addition to his description in the "Lettre du voyant" of how the *voyant* would destroy himself, there are indications throughout his poetry that he knew that his poetic method was undermining his physical, emotional and mental health; furthermore, he seemed to realize that he could not achieve the transcendence he craved.

AFRICA

From his twentieth year until his death, Rimbaud traveled across Europe, often on foot, and worked in Cyprus, Africa and Egypt. In 1876 he joined the Dutch colonial army in order to reach Java, but deserted in Batavia. One year later he wrote to the American Consul in Bremen to inquire about enlisting in the United States Navy; Rimbaud seems not to have included a return address, however. He worked for Viannay, Mazeran, Bardey and Company in Aden (in present-day Southern Yemen) and Harar (in Abyssinia, modern Ethiopia), dealing in skins and coffee. During his wanderings he studied the Arabic and Abyssinian languages and explored the Ogaden area in Ethiopia, which, until then, had never been

---

4. H. de Bouillane de Lacoste, *Rimbaud et le problème des Illuminations* (Paris, 1949).

Rimbaud in Abyssinia (ca. 1883).
(French Cultural Services, New York)

investigated by a European. His report on this region was published in the *Comptes Rendus des Séances de la Société de Géographie* (Paris, 1884). In 1887 he tried to make a fortune by selling guns to King Menelik II of Shoa (now the province in central Ethiopia whose capital is Addis Ababa). But during this dangerous expedition, which lasted over five months, the poet-turned-entrepreneur lost sixty per cent of his capital and had to devote twenty-one months to rearranging his affairs.

Some have claimed that in Africa Rimbaud tried to become rich by participating in the slave trade; however, in the poet's letter of December 3, 1885, in which he described the slave traffic, the "only" successful native commerce in the region of Tadjourah, Rimbaud wrote his family: "Don't go around thinking that I've become a slave-trader." He then described how he would sell guns to Menelik II.

Rimbaud's life as a colonial reflects the thinking developed in his poetry. Life in France would probably have been too dull, too oppressive for him, but travel in Europe and Africa seems to have provided the outlet necessary for his energy after he had stopped writing. While trying to make money as a businessman in Abyssinia, he was, in a way, adapting to reality and its accepted values: work, wealth and a kind of "established happiness." But by living in Africa, Rimbaud did not have to make a complete concession to European life. He could continue to wander and to dream. At one point he even imagined that after his travels he would like to settle down and have "at least one son," whom he would rear to be "a famous engineer, a man powerful and rich through science" (May 6, 1883).

Often, however, Rimbaud was not content in Africa. Living in these "atrocious climates," he wrote from Harar on May 25, 1881, he is "forced" to exhaust himself with vexations that are "as violent as they are absurd." In some of his letters the former *voyant* who satirized European colonials in *Democracy* even sounds strangely like the ethnocentric men he once mocked. For example, on Janu-

Rimbaud several days before his death. Drawing by his sister Isabelle. (French Cultural Services, New York)

ary 15, 1885, Rimbaud calls Aden "this dirty country"; elsewhere he denounces the Africans as "stupid" (February 20, 1891) and "savage" (September 10, 1884). Still, his letters (like *Bad Blood* of *A Season in Hell*) reveal his basic ambivalence toward the Africans and their continent, for on February 25, 1890, he wrote that the African Negroes are not as bad as the "white Negroes of the so-called civilized countries." It is simply a question of degree, he insists, and actually the Abyssinians are "less wicked." [5] Although Rimbaud was often not really happy in Africa, he probably would

5. For a study of Rimbaud's ambivalent attitude toward Africa, see Enid H. Rhodes, "Under the Spell of Africa: Poems and Letters of Arthur Rimbaud Inspired by the Dark Continent," *French Review*, Vol. XLIV (Special Issue, No. 2, Winter 1971), 20–28.

have been even less happy in France. "Aden," he wrote to his mother and sister in France, is "the most boring place in the world, after, however, the one where you live" (September 22, 1880). Thus, in his life as in his poetry, Rimbaud neither completely capitulated to ordinary existence, nor completely escaped from it. The unfortunate thing is that in order for him to reconcile himself with reality, he had to repudiate his poetic method and, with it, his poetry.

In 1891 Rimbaud returned to France with a tumor, possibly of syphilitic origin, in his right knee. On November 10, 1891, the former poet, then thirty-seven years old, died in Marseilles completely unaware that in Paris his major works were being published and studied. Verlaine, like the Foolish Virgin of *A Season in Hell* who was "never jealous" of her infernal companion, had introduced Rimbaud's writing to the public. The older poet devoted a chapter to Rimbaud in his book *Les Poètes maudits* (Vanier, 1884) and edited the first edition of the *Illuminations*, published by *La Vogue* in 1886. *A Season in Hell*, first printed in Brussels in 1873 (Alliance typographique, Poot et Cie), did not become widely known until eighteen years later, when Verlaine wrote the introduction for Vanier (*Poèmes, Les Illuminations, Une Saison en enfer*. Notice par Paul Verlaine, Vanier, 1891 [6]).

INFLUENCE

Rimbaud's revolutionary artistic achievements — his new poetic language and form, including his use of free verse; his concept of the *voyant*; and his desire to change life through poetry — should be examined in the context of innovative predecessors. Gérard de Nerval, for example, tried to capture in his writings his experience of the ineffable; Victor Hugo depicted richly imaginative visions

6. This date appears in the Vanier edition in the Yale University Library. The Pléiade edition of Rimbaud's works (Paris, 1963), however, gives 1892 as the Vanier publication date (p. 879).

("*Les Misérables* is a true poem," Rimbaud wrote in the "Lettre du voyant"); and Charles Baudelaire proclaimed in *The Voyage* (*Le Voyage*) that his goal was "to find the new." In his poetic form, as well, Rimbaud is indebted to his artistic forebears. Poetic prose by Chateaubriand and Lamennais led to the more condensed prose poem developed by Aloysius Bertrand and Baudelaire.

Rimbaud hoped to surpass Baudelaire, his most important precursor, both in poetic form and in language. Whereas Baudelaire concluded *The Flowers of Evil* (*Les Fleurs du mal*) with his wish to find "the new," the younger writer began his poetic quest with the same idea. And so, going beyond Baudelaire, Rimbaud created the poem-illumination, a synesthetic explosion of sound, color, emotion and perpetual movement. Through his new language and form, Rimbaud forged a revolutionary world of sensuous wonders combining the real and the unreal in visionary and hallucinatory projections.

"Flash . . . of a meteor, ignited without motive other than his own presence, descended alone and dying," was Mallarmé's description of Rimbaud.[7] This "meteor" had a considerable influence on poets who succeeded him.

By freeing French poetry from the strict rules of rhyme and meter, Rimbaud was a precursor of writers like Jules Laforgue, Gustave Kahn and Jean Moréas. The *Illuminations*, including two of the first free verse poems in French, *Seascape* and *Movement*, were originally published in Kahn's Symbolist review, *La Vogue*. During the last fifteen years of the nineteenth century, in fact, some of the Symbolists acclaimed Rimbaud, whose major works were then being printed. His sonnet *Vowels* (*Voyelles*) became a manifesto of color-hearing and verbal instrumentation for many writers. The assignment of a specific color to each vowel was a particularly striking example of his practice of synesthesia.

Far more important than Rimbaud's effect on the Symbolists

7. Stéphane Mallarmé, Letter to Harrison Rhodes, April 1896, *Oeuvres complètes* (Paris: Pléiade, 1945), p. 512.

was his influence on the Dadaists and the Surrealists. The Dadaists, in their glorification of total negation, their explosions of anarchy and their rebellion against traditional esthetic values, idealized Rimbaud and Lautréamont. The Surrealists admired Rimbaud's vision of poetry as a magical means for discovering the unknown; his reliance on reverie; his violent images; his desire to liberate his ego and his art from all restrictions; his searching to discover the sources of language. For these writers Rimbaud was a poet-alchemist, a visionary maker of images who, by deranging his senses, sought to uncover the unconscious sources of the poetic imagination. In addition, they, like the Symbolists, were fascinated by the legend of his life: his rebellions, his renunciation of poetry and his self-imposed exile in Africa. "Rimbaud is a Surrealist in the practice of life and elsewhere," André Breton wrote in his first *Manifesto of Surrealism* in 1924.[8]

Other writers — Paul Claudel and Jacques Rivière — have found in Rimbaud a source of religious inspiration. Claudel wrote that Rimbaud was the human factor that led him back to his Catholic faith.

Arthur Rimbaud's violence, his revolt, his acceptance of evil and vice as instruments for self-liberation and transcendence also call for comparisons with other writers he inspired: André Gide (especially in *The Terrestrial Foods* [*Les Nourritures terrestres*]); Henry Miller; Hart Crane, who used Rimbaud's words "It can only be the end of the world, ahead" as the epigraph for *White Buildings;* Aimé Césaire; and Jean Genet.

A SEASON IN HELL

A Season in Hell combines autobiography and lucid self-appraisal with vision and hallucination. In this work a first person narrator with multiple voices and personalities dramatizes his struggles to overcome his sufferings and to establish a footing for himself in a

8. André Breton, *Manifestes du surréalisme* (Paris: Gallimard, n.d.), p. 39.

precarious balance between reality and reverie. The last paragraphs of each of the nine sections of this dramatic narrative become starting points for further thought and imagery.

In the introduction, beginning in medias res, the speaker reveals that he would like to recover a glorious past which is now lost — lost because of his rebellions against "Beauty," justice, hope and life; and lost for reasons he cannot comprehend. With the following words he begins his drama of self-portrayal and self-judgment: "In former times, if I remember rightly, my life was a feast at which all hearts opened up, at which all wines flowed." While the opening expression carries him into his mythical past, the inserted phrase, "if I remember rightly," reveals, on the other hand, the author's clear and critical observation of his own poetic fancy. Here a fundamental pattern of A Season in Hell emerges. As soon as the poet describes his dreams or desires, another speaker, the voice in reality (like the "I" who observed the poet's other selves in the "Lettre du voyant"), often interrupts him. As the introduction closes, the narrator explains that what follows is his "notebook of a soul condemned to hell."

Bad Blood portrays the poet's explorations of his origins, his escapist desires and his continuing battles against reality. Symbolizing his Gallic and peasant heritage, his "bad blood" makes him a member of "an inferior race." The narrator here both derides and praises his pagan ancestors. Attempting to flee from his background, he portrays himself in other existences: he is an African, a pilgrim to the Holy Land, a mercenary, or a leper; he is a ferocious invalid returned home from torrid countries. When back in reality, he is "cursed," or, as he says sarcastically, "saved." On a battlefield in the last section of Bad Blood, the protagonist suddenly declares that he does not want to die: in a final exclamation he says that he will get used to "the French way of life," which he calls ironically "the path of honor." From this point on, A Season in Hell recounts the drama of that decision.

During the torments of his Night of Hell the poet hallucinates,

judges and condemns. Suffocating, writhing with the "violence of the venom," he exclaims that this inferno is actually his "life!" He is damned because of his religious rearing: "Hell cannot assail pagans," he says. But the poet burning in these infernal flames also delights in his very agonies. "Ecstasy, nightmare, sleep in a nest of flames," he calls out. In this section too, the protean protagonist reveals that his ambitions were, and still remain, Luciferian. At one point he even usurps the role of Jesus, whose language he mimics. Still, *Night of Hell* is the beginning of his purgation. After the hallucinations in the abyss of his anguish, he seeks to understand, and therefore to surmount, his suffering.

The two *Deliriums* illustrate the narrator's struggles in the realms of love and art. Carrying connotations of wild enthusiasm, hallucination, intoxication and insanity, the word "deliriums" highlights the author's interpretation of his endeavors: he both glorifies and denigrates his undertakings.

The epitome of the poet's quest for transcendent love appears in *Deliriums I*, where the Infernal Bridegroom, a self-characterization of Rimbaud and a parody, probably, of Jesus as the Heavenly Bridegroom, proclaims: "I don't like women. Love has to be invented over again, that's known." His mistress, the weak and tearful Foolish Virgin, is a delineation of Verlaine, as well as a likely caricature of the foolish virgins in the parable in the Gospel of Matthew.

In *Deliriums I* the Foolish Virgin presents a portrait of her masochistic, sadistic, but sometimes gentle lover. While she is his "slave," she wonders if this "Demon" who "was practically a child" possesses "secrets for *transforming life*." But the fact that she says her lover "pretended to be enlightened about everything" discloses that she (as well as Rimbaud) knows that the Infernal Bridegroom does not possess the powers he claims as his. Even in their love relationship both characters are isolated, alienated. The Foolish Virgin is "sure of never entering" her infernal partner's world, and he, of course, recognizes this.

L'Éternité

Elle est retrouvée.
Quoi ? — L'éternité.
C'est la mer allée
Avec le soleil

Âme sentinelle,
Murmurons l'aveu
De la nuit si nulle
Et du jour en feu.

Des humains suffrages
Des communs élans
Là tu te dégages
Et voles selon.

Puisque de vous seules,
Braises de satin,
Le Devoir s'exhale
Sans qu'on dise : enfin.

Là pas d'espérance,
Nul orietur.
Science avec patience,
Le supplice est sûr.

Elle est retrouvée.
Quoi ? — L'éternité.
(C'est la mer allée)
Avec le soleil

Mai '72

Manuscript of the 1872 version of Rimbaud's poem *L'Eternité* (*Eternity*). Rimbaud revised this poem a year later and used it in *Deliriums II* of *A Season in Hell* (see page 86). (French Cultural Services, New York)

Announcing now that it is his turn to speak, the poet in *Deliriums II* dramatizes and condemns, for the most part, his "Alchemy of the Word," his exalted and heretical ambition to surpass life through poetry, to transform the Word, the Logos, into the alchemist's goal: gold.

Here, language is a source and a symbol of the poet's intoxication with words, sounds, rhythms, images and dreams. But he alternates in his words and implied tones between prideful glorification and sarcastic rejection of his undertaking; this is evident, for example, when he describes how he regarded language. Referring to his sonnet *Vowels*, he exclaims: "I invented the color of the vowels!" Soon, however, he bridles his enthusiasm by mocking the hopes expressed in the "Lettre du voyant," for now he says that he "flattered" himself into thinking he had devised "a poetic language" which would one day be "accessible . . . to all the senses." But suddenly he attacks those who did not — who would not or who could not — understand his new poetic language: he says he "withheld the translation." And in the words which follow he reveals how much he still admires the grandeur of his undertaking. He claims that he "recorded the inexpressible"; he "wrote down silences, nights"; he "determined vertigoes." The poems he quotes immediately thereafter ("Remote from birds . . ." and "At four in the morning . . .") justify his esthetic claims,[9] while also treating many of the major themes of *Deliriums II*: isolation, alchemy, impotence, thirst, hallucination, love, suffering, intoxication, darkness and light. Of course, right after these poems he mocks himself again, calling his achievements "old tricks of poetry."

9. Although some critics claim that in *Deliriums II* Rimbaud quoted his poems of 1872 carelessly from memory because he no longer admired them, others feel that the poet took pains to revise these earlier compositions. See Emilie Noulet's demonstration of how Rimbaud improved these poems in "Sur La 'Chanson de la plus haute tour'" and "Le Poème d'une larme" in *Suites: Mallarmé, Rimbaud, Valéry* (Paris, 1964), pp. 132–46 and 147–59.

The narrator in *Deliriums II* realizes that in the pursuit of his poetic method, his search for happiness and for the "unknown," he was destroying himself. In musical cadences, he portrays how he almost died:

> My health was threatened. Terror developed. I fell into sleeps of several days' duration, and when up, I continued the saddest dreams. I was ripe for death, and by a road of dangers my weakness led me to the ends of the world and of Cimmeria, the home of darkness and of whirlwinds.

At the end of *Deliriums II* the narrator says that he knows "today how to hail beauty." This "beauty," probably that which pleases ordinary people, seems to be the antithesis of the narrator's idealized "Beauty," written with a capital letter, of the introduction. While he now knows how to accommodate to mundane tastes and reality, he appears less than enthusiastic.

But dreams come to the rescue. In *The Impossible* the poet depicts his reveries of escape to an Eden-like East; nevertheless the title expresses the futility of his desires. In this emotionally charged section, conflicts occur: between the dreamer who invented an extraordinary childhood and the realist who talks in a derisory tone; between two voices in the present, one which seeks transcendence and another which comments bitterly upon the former's desires. As the tension mounts, the protagonist realizes more and more that he is a creature of Western culture. That culture, he says with distaste, is populated by "polite" hypocrites who "disgust one another." Suddenly, as in other moments of despair, he dreams of wisdom, purity and God. " — Through the spirit one reaches God!" his visionary voice exclaims. "Harrowing misfortune!" his bitter voice counters, quelling the other's ecstasy.

During *The Flash of Lightning* the protagonist experiences moments of hope: hope in human toil, science (knowledge?), religion, dreams, escape and rebellion. Such illuminations are transient,

however. Rejecting confessors and martyrs as part of his "foul" rearing, and death and work as poor solutions to his problems, he concludes this section by wondering if eternity would now be lost to him.

Then, as if waking up from a nightmare in *Morning*, he finds resurgent courage in a social vision of a new religion. Asserting that he has now finished the account of his hell, he proclaims in prophetic tones the world he foresees: he hopes to go "beyond the shores and the mountains" to hail a new religion defined in terms of "new work . . . new wisdom . . . [and] the end of superstition." "The song of the heavens, the procession of peoples!" he exclaims. As the scene closes, the speaker tries to encourage men, even if all men are the "slaves" of reality, to have some hope. "Slaves," he says, "let us not blaspheme life."

His attempts to adjust to ordinary existence continue in *Farewell*. Through this final section the dreamer and the realist dialogue frequently. While it is probably the former, remembering his past, who says: "I have created all festivals, all triumphs, all dramas," in all likelihood it is the self-critical realist who explains that he "tried to invent new flowers, new stars, new flesh, new tongues," and who adds that he "believed . . . [he] acquired supernatural powers." Suddenly the sarcastic speaker erupts in exclamations: "Well! I must bury my imagination and my memories! A great glory as an artist and storyteller swept away!" In this one paragraph the narrator's tones have proceeded from dream-vision through judgment to self-condemnation.

Continuing in the next paragraph, he mocks not only himself, but all of reality also. "I! I who called myself a seer or an angel, exempt from all morality," he begins, thereby lauding his extraordinary past, while pretending to denounce it. His utterance ends in a burst of irony: "I am restored to the earth, with a duty to seek, and rugged reality to embrace! Peasant!" "Peasant!" he calls himself, for he is, by birth, a peasant, but the protagonist

knows, even here, that he is far more than that. The one-word exclamation intensifies both his self-contempt and his scorn for the social system that defines him as a peasant. At once he accepts and assails reality.

Yet it is the poet dreaming of an illuminating new dawn and "splendid cities," and not the realist awkwardly embracing "rugged reality," who utters the final words in *Farewell*. It will be "permissible for me *to possess truth in one soul and one body*," he says. The poet has managed to accept reality and the present only by escaping into reveries of an idealized future in which he will be able to grasp a new vision: embodied truth.

A *Season in Hell* represents Rimbaud's torments during a crucial stage of his life: the period when he practiced the method described in the "Lettre du voyant," and the time of his physical, emotional, moral and spiritual development. While he claims that his "hell" is the Christian one, "the one whose gates the son of man opened," he also reveals that his inferno is actually his life. And he is in this hell, he says, because of the many conflicting elements in his heritage (his Gallic, peasant and Christian ancestry) and in his chosen life style, including his poetic method, his delight in ecstatic anguish and intoxications, his quest for transcendence through love and art, his dreams of fleeing from the West, and his continuing rebellion against the hypocrisies of bourgeois life in nineteenth-century France. A *Season in Hell* is the poet's poignant confession and dramatic narrative of his struggle to adapt to reality. Through his changing tones, voices, words and images, the protagonist reveals his ambivalent vision of himself, his homeland, his art and all life. The end of the drama is not a conclusion; rather, it is another beginning in his voyage away from darkness and into light.

THE ILLUMINATIONS

"The word 'ILLUMINATIONS' is English and means . . . *coloured plates*," Verlaine wrote in his preface to the first edition of Rimbaud's *Illuminations*.[10] In addition to these colorful and graphical impressions, the word suggests flashes of inspiration and explosions of light, but also the possibility of ensuing darkness.

In the forty-two poems of this group, movement occurs in a continually changing present, or against a rapidly evolving backdrop of commingling eras. Places enlarge, diminish or conjoin. Realms of being interpenetrate, creating surrealistic disorientations, linking the concrete and the abstract, the real and the unreal: "people play cards at the bottom of the pond." In the two free-verse poems, *Movement* and *Seascape*, horizontal and vertical motions become hallucinatory in their oscillating modulations, combining whirling and disparate elements.

Frequent metamorphoses of places and of persons accentuate the fluidity and the fragility of the poet's world. The narrator is the "saint," the "scholar" and the "pedestrian" in *Childhood IV*; he adds that he could well be the "child." At his "lady's house" in *Bottom*, the speaker becomes sadder, more awkward and more pathetic with each incarnation: he changes from a "large blue-gray bird" to a "big bear" whose fur is "gray with grief," and finally, like Shakespeare's Bottom in *A Midsummer Night's Dream*, he becomes an "ass."

In the world of the *Illuminations* Rimbaud's words simultaneously design, alter and destroy the universe they describe. Creation bears within it the seeds of destruction in *After the Flood*, *Historic Evening* and *Being Beauteous*, for example. In the last-mentioned

10. Paul Verlaine, "Préface de la première édition des *Illuminations*" (1886) in Arthur Rimbaud, *Poèmes, Les Illuminations, Une Saison en enfer* (Paris: Vanier, 1891), p. v.

poem, "the Vision, in the making" is also described in process of ruination. The poet's numerous references to theater, magic and fairyland accentuate his awareness that he is constructing artificial worlds which may vanish in a moment.

At least four types of designs are discernible in the *Illumina-tions:* a circular pattern, a quasi-circular framework, an illuminated picture, and a disintegrating or vanishing vision. In *Barbarian* and *Common Nocturne,* the circular compositions, the last line echoes the first. These poems reveal a changing, but somehow static, world where words that echo ever-evolving dreams form ever-revolving prisons: the poet is caught in this wonderful and terrible universe. Poems like *Pageant, Devotion* and *Anguish* have a quasi-circular design in which the last lines, without actually repeating the first, direct the reader back to the beginning, thereby encouraging a new interpretation of the work. Such poems as *Flowers, Seascape, Ruts, Mystic* and *Antique* are illuminated pictures which create worlds of tantalizing beauty, or glimpses of beauty and horror. In other poems, *Being Beauteous, Dawn, The Bridges* and *Tale,* for example, the illumination appears only to disintegrate or disappear before the poet's eyes. All these designs shape universes in perpetual motion.

Along with continual metamorphoses, creation and destruction, theater, magic and fairyland, other motifs recur frequently in the *Illuminations.* Among them are: childhood, voyages, dreams, a flood, death, love, woman, the poet's omnipotence and impotence, hope and despair, religion, newness, cities, arctic chaos, nature and art.

Love, in all its contradictory aspects, is a dominant theme. Rimbaud exclaims, "Love! strength! — loftier than all joys and glories!"; but love in these poems also involves suffering, frustration and loneliness. Possession in *Dawn* is only momentary, and the "hour of the 'dear body' and 'dear heart' " is "a bore" in *Childhood I.* The fact that the narrator dreams of "the loved one neither tormenting

nor tormented" in *Vigils I* intimates that he expects lovers to be one or the other, or both. In several poems, including *To a Reason, Tale* and *Genie*, the poet dreams of a marvelous "new love" and a revolutionary "charity," which would combine spiritual and erotic pleasures. The Prince in *Tale* foresees "astonishing revolutions in love"; he longs for desire and its simultaneous satisfaction. Personifying the poet's cravings, the Genie of *Genie* "is love, perfect and reinvented measure, marvelous and unforeseen reason, and eternity." But the poet is always disappointed. *Tale* closes with these disheartened words: "Masterly music disappoints our desire," and *Genie* ends with the realization that people on earth are separated from the Genie of love.

Rebelling against ordinary life, the poet in the *Illuminations* craves release. He dreams of escaping into barbaric splendors or visionary cities. These seemingly contradictory desires actually complement each other by reinforcing his rejection of bourgeois society; naturally, he is never satisfied. Despite numerous marvels in the two works entitled *Cities*, many disruptive forces operate. In the one beginning "The official acropolis . . . ," the grandiose style of the city is actually grotesque, and in "What cities these are!", there are "avalanches," "the collapse of apotheoses" and a sea that "grows somber sometimes with fatal flashes." The author seems both attracted and repelled by his vision of modern civilization. The last three images of *City*, personifying Death, despondent Love and Crime, symbolize the forces of despair in contemporary cities.

Intoxication is another way in which Rimbaud dreams of escaping from oppressive reality. Little is really known about what intoxicants he used, the quantities he consumed, or when. Throughout his poems and letters, he speaks of wine, beer, liquors and absinthe. In *Morning of Drunkenness* he is probably referring to hashish when he writes about "the time of the ASSASSINS," because the word "assassins," derived from the Arabic *hashshāshīn*, means "eaters of hashish." Exalting the "Good," the "Beautiful" and himself, the

speaker begins by exclaiming: "O *my* Good! O *my* Beautiful!" His mind and his emotions are thrilled with the "marvelous body, for the first time!" Still, the knowledge that intoxicants are also "poisons" haunts him: "This poison will remain in all our veins even when, with the changing fanfare, we shall be surrendered to our former disharmony." And while exulting in his ecstatic tortures, he reveals his awareness that his "little vigil of drunkenness, sanctified!" is propelling him directly to dissolution and death. Yet in this poem he asserts his "faith in the poison."

It is interesting to compare Ernest Delahaye's description of how Rimbaud reacted to hashish with the dream-vision in *Morning of Drunkenness*. Delahaye relates how he and Verlaine visited Rimbaud in Paris. The poet who wanted to make himself a *voyant* had taken hashish and was asleep on a hotel bench. When awakened and asked about his experience, he said that he had seen "nothing at all . . . some white moons, some black moons, that were chasing each other." "In other words," Delahaye adds, "the famous drug had disturbed his stomach, given him dizziness, exhaustion: an 'artificial paradise' totally bungled." [11]

The narrator's tone in the *Illuminations*, as in *A Season in Hell*, is frequently caustic, sarcastic, ironic: the "I" of the "Lettre du voyant" often observes, judges, denounces. For example, in *Democracy*, while the speaker seems to assume the role of a white soldier who is probably in Africa, the poet turns the full force of his irony against this very colonial who works "at the service of the most monstrous industrial or military exploitations." Still, when the poet calls the country to be conquered the "foul landscape," he also betrays his bourgeois repugnance for this uncivilized land. By means of this double-edged irony, Rimbaud reveals his ambivalence toward both Africa and the West — and therefore, toward himself. Through the interplay of sarcastic tones, *Democracy* assails the world it creates, as well as the real world.

11. Ernest Delahaye, *Souvenirs familiers à propos de Rimbaud, Verlaine, Germain Nouveau* (Paris, 1925), p. 162.

In all of the *Illuminations*, the structures, tones and images reveal tensions between the poet's dreams and reality, between ecstasy and anguish, between hope and despair. Frequently the words and the way they are used function in counterpoint, the one playing against the other.

Although the poet feels that art "disappoints our desire," as he says in *Tale*, there is a strange and poignant beauty in the *Illuminations*, in their universe of evanescent forms in continual evolution, a world always hovering between creation and ruination. Just because "we cannot at once grasp" the poet's vision, which he calls "this eternity" in *Morning of Drunkenness*, we are enticed to return again and again, each time with a deeper appreciation, to their beauty and their ever-enchanting ambiguity.

A Note on Translation

A translation is no translation, he said, unless it will give you the music of a poem along with the words of it.

JOHN MILLINGTON SYNGE (*The Aran Islands*)

I flattered myself on devising a poetic language accessible, one day or another, to all the senses. I withheld the translation.

ARTHUR RIMBAUD (*Deliriums II*)

The word "translation" is derived from *translatus*, the past participle of the Latin verb *transferre*, which means "to carry over or across," "to transfer," "to transport," "to convey," "to translate." When a translation is successful, the finished product may well make one recall this Latin verb, for the essence of the original work is carried over into the new version. As Synge's statement indicates, the tone colors and rhythms of the second language recapture the inspiring music of the first.

Quintilian recommends the practice of translation for those who wish to learn to write with ease and skill. In translating, the ancient rhetorician says, a writer can use the best words available in his own language (*"hos transferentibus verbis uti optimis licit,"* *Institutionis Oratoriae*, X, 5). My experience with Rimbaud's poems confirms Quintilian's observation. One who undertakes to translate the work of a great writer serves an invaluable apprenticeship to a master. In the effort to render the author's thought, emotion and music in equivalent language, the translator learns both the science and the art of expression. Precision and power develop in this process of re-creating the text.

Rimbaud's tongue-in-cheek comment that he "withheld the translation" of his poetry sometimes would come to haunt me — or to taunt me — when I found myself struggling with an especially difficult passage. His poetic language, as he himself says, seeks to express "the inexpressible," determine "vertigoes," record "silences." Indeed, Rimbaud has tempted many translators before me and will continue to challenge others after me.

This translation of A Season in Hell and the Illuminations is the result of countless hours of study and appraisal of Rimbaud's words, ideas, sounds and rhythms. His punctuation and word order, too, were carefully noted and, wherever possible, retained. I hope that my translation will enable those who are not well versed in the French language and literature to understand something of the brilliance of this amazing poet and the relevance of his ideas to today's world.

Certain difficulties beset me in the course of this work. For example, the words esprit and science both convey two important, but different, ideas in French. Esprit can mean spirit or mind; science means knowledge or science. At times I have chosen one:

Mon esprit, prends garde.	My spirit, take care.
. . . depuis cette déclaration de la science, le christianisme. . . .	. . . since that declaration of knowledge, Christianity. . . .

In different contexts, however, I have had to select the other meaning:

Je parvins à faire s'évanouir dans mon esprit toute l'espérance humaine.	I succeeded in erasing from my mind all human hope.
La science, la nouvelle noblesse!	Science, the new nobility!

I wish there were English words which could convey these double implications. In one passage in *Bad Blood* I have used "knowledge" as the generic term, which may include "science" in its meaning:

L'amour divin seul octroie les clefs de la science.	Divine love alone confers the keys of knowledge.

"Mind" and "spirit," however, are usually pointedly differentiated in English. In *The Impossible*, where Rimbaud is talking about his dreams of a pagan paradise in the East, I have used the word "spirit" to translate *l'esprit*, but this, of course, leaves out the kind of word play implying that religion is a rational thing. ("My spirit [mind], take care. No violent resolutions on salvation.") After all, only a few pages earlier in *Bad Blood*, Rimbaud described Christianity as "the reasonable song of angels." And in order to adapt, he said he would retain his "place at the top of this angelic ladder of common sense."

There were other problems of interpretation. One, for example, concerns the implied meaning of words. When Rimbaud talks about the "incorrigible convict," he says: "je voyais *avec son idée.*" I have rendered this as: "I saw *with his fancy.*" Another involves a synonym of *reason* in English. I have translated "dès l'âge de raison" in *Bad Blood* as "from the years of discretion" rather than as "from the age of reason," because the latter expression immediately brings to mind the eighteenth century, whereas in this passage Rimbaud is talking about his "vice" (probably a reference to his homosexuality or to his rebellious nature) which has been tormenting him not since the epoch of Voltaire, Diderot, Montesquieu and Rousseau, but rather since the time when he became aware that his urges were considered "sinful."

Occasionally, in order to clarify Rimbaud's highly compressed idea, I have expanded his expression. Thus I have rendered "mon

carnet de damné" as "my notebook of a soul condemned to hell."
In order to translate "La dernière innocence et la dernière timidité,"
I have added words to make the meaning more intelligible in
English: "The last shred of innocence and the last vestige of shy-
ness."

I have made every effort to keep Rimbaud's word order so that
the flow of his thought may proceed as it does in the French. If,
however, the translated version would suggest a Frenchman trying
to speak English, I rearranged the sentence to make it run smoothly
in English. "C'est très-certain, c'est oracle, ce que je dis" was therefore transposed as: "What I say is quite certain, it's an oracle."

Although my primary concern has been to be faithful to Rimbaud's meaning, I have still tried to utilize some of his poetic
devices. Thus, I have attempted to reproduce his alliterative effects,
but I have never sacrificed sense in an effort to mimic sound per se.
A few examples will suffice:

Plus tard, les délices de la damna-tion seront plus profondes.	Later, the delights of damnation will be deeper.
. . . je suis prêt pour la perfec-tion . . . Orgueil.	. . . I am prepared for perfection . . . Pride.
. . . l'homme . . . se prouve les évidences, se gonfle du plaisir de répéter ces preuves. . . .	. . . man . . . proves obvious ideas to himself, puffs himself up with the pleasure of repeating these proofs. . . .

In addition to alliteration, which occurs throughout A Season
in Hell, Rimbaud used both rhythm and rhyme in the lyric poems
of Deliriums II. These pieces, which scholars call Rimbaud's
"Derniers Vers," were originally written during the spring and
summer of 1872, that is, one year before the poet began A Season
in Hell. They are quoted with some variations in the later work.

In my renditions of these poems, I have tried to approximate

Rimbaud's poetic sounds and rhythms, without sacrificing his thoughts. I frequently had to forgo rhyme. "Remote from birds, from flocks . . ." has an unusual rhyme scheme in the French: *abcb abac dedee*. It is composed of hendecasyllabic lines, except for the eighth, which is an alexandrine. In this poem Rimbaud used some significant enjambment: e.g. "cette bruyère/Entourée"; and "loin de ma case/Chérie," which, by reducing the number of end-stopped lines, lets the words flow more freely and makes the rhyme seem almost internal. Rimbaud actually did use some internal rhyme in this poem ("oiseaux . . . troupeaux"). He also created echoes by repeating certain vowel sounds: for example, /wa/ recurs in "oiseaux," "villageoises," "bois," "noisetiers," "voix." In translating this poem, I have used alliteration (" — A storm arose and stalked the sky"); assonance, when I found it feasible to do so without altering Rimbaud's meaning or violating English syntax (e.g. inn: virgin); and iambic pentameter (except for variations in lines six and seven, and in the last line, which is trochaic) to suggest the rhythm. Since the unit of rhythm is the metrical foot in English and the syllable in French, my scansion could not conform exactly to Rimbaud's. The English version of "At four in the morning, in summertime . . ." employs a predominantly iambic beat, but not always, since Rimbaud's rhythm in this poem is extremely uneven. In *Song of the Highest Tower*, I used iambic tetrameter for the most part to render Rimbaud's pentasyllabic verses, which appear throughout the poem except for the six-syllable second line of the refrain and the four-syllable "Des sales mouches."

Rimbaud's five or six years of poetic creation have had an extraordinary influence on modern poetry, not only in France, but in other countries also. His works helped to inspire poetic Symbolism, Dadaism and Surrealism. Translating this remarkable poet, though he lived over a hundred years ago, has been like communing with someone who is active in the vanguard today. This is so because Rimbaud's poetry is not merely an exercise in daring language

and beautiful imagery; it is the intellectual, emotional and spiritual struggle of a brilliant and tormented writer who is perpetually exploring himself in his baffling, elusive relation to childhood, adulthood and eternity. His poetry has also had a liberating effect. Rimbaud is the one who declares in the "Lettre du voyant": "While waiting, let us ask the *poet* for the *new*, — ideas and forms." And that, along with the impetus and the inspiration to continue searching, is precisely what he has given us.

Une Saison en Enfer

A Season in Hell

Jadis, si je me souviens bien, ma vie était un festin où s'ouvraient tous les cœurs, où tous les vins coulaient.

Un soir, j'ai assis la Beauté sur mes genoux. — Et je l'ai trouvée amère. — Et je l'ai injuriée.

Je me suis armé contre la justice.

Je me suis enfui. O sorcières, ô misère, ô haine, c'est à vous que mon trésor a été confié!

Je parvins à faire s'évanouir dans mon esprit toute l'espérance humaine. Sur toute joie pour l'étrangler j'ai fait le bond sourd de la bête féroce.

J'ai appelé les bourreaux pour, en périssant, mordre la crosse de leurs fusils. J'ai appelé les fléaux, pour m'étouffer avec le sable, le sang. Le malheur a été mon dieu. Je me suis allongé dans la boue. Je me suis séché à l'air du crime. Et j'ai joué de bons tours à la folie.

Et le printemps m'a apporté l'affreux rire de l'idiot.

Or, tout dernièrement m'étant trouvé sur le point de faire le dernier *couac!* j'ai songé à rechercher la clef du festin ancien, où je reprendrais peut-être appétit.

La charité est cette clef. — Cette inspiration prouve que j'ai rêvé!

« Tu resteras hyène, etc. . . », se récrie le démon qui me couronna de si aimables pavots. « Gagne la mort avec tous tes appétits, et ton égoïsme et tous les péchés capitaux. »

Ah! j'en ai trop pris: — Mais, cher Satan, je vous en conjure, une prunelle moins irritée! et en attendant les quelques petites lâchetés en retard, vous qui aimez dans l'écrivain l'absence des facultés descriptives ou instructives, je vous détache ces quelques hideux feuillets de mon carnet de damné.

In former times, if I remember rightly, my life was a feast at which all hearts opened up, at which all wines flowed.

One evening, I seated Beauty on my knees. — And I found her bitter. — And I railed against her.

I armed myself against justice.

I fled. O sorceresses, O misery, O hate, it's to you that my treasure was confided!

I succeeded in erasing from my mind all human hope. Upon every joy, in order to strangle it, I made the muffled leap of the wild beast.

I summoned the executioners in order to bite the butts of their guns as I was dying. I summoned the plagues, to suffocate myself with sand, with blood. Misfortune was my god. I stretched myself out in the mud. I dried myself in the air of crime. And I played some fine tricks on madness.

And spring brought me the horrifying laughter of the idiot.

Now, quite recently finding myself on the point of sounding my last *squawk!* I thought of searching for the key to the ancient feast, where I might possibly recover my appetite.

Charity is this key. — This inspiration proves that I've been dreaming!

"You'll remain a hyena, etc. . . . ," exclaims the demon who crowned me with such lovely poppies. "Meet death with all your lusts, and your selfishness and all the deadly sins."

Ah! I've collected too many of them: — But, dear Satan, I implore you, an eye that is less angry! and while awaiting the few little belated cowardly deeds, you who admire in a writer the absence of descriptive or instructive talents, I tear out for you these few hideous leaves from my notebook of a soul condemned to hell.

Mauvais Sang

J'ai de mes ancêtres gaulois l'œil bleu blanc, la cervelle étroite, et la maladresse dans la lutte. Je trouve mon habillement aussi barbare que le leur. Mais je ne beurre pas ma chevelure.

Les Gaulois étaient les écorcheurs de bêtes, les brûleurs d'herbes les plus ineptes de leur temps.

D'eux, j'ai: l'idolâtrie et l'amour du sacrilège; — oh! tous les vices, colère, luxure, — magnifique, la luxure; — surtout mensonge et paresse.

J'ai horreur de tous les métiers. Maîtres et ouvriers, tous paysans, ignobles. La main à plume vaut la main à charrue. — Quel siècle à mains! — Je n'aurai jamais ma main. Après, la domesticité mène trop loin. L'honnêteté de la mendicité me navre. Les criminels dégoûtent comme des châtrés: moi, je suis intact, et ça m'est égal.

Mais! qui a fait ma langue perfide tellement, qu'elle ait guidé et sauvegardé jusqu'ici ma paresse? Sans me servir pour vivre même de mon corps, et plus oisif que le crapaud, j'ai vécu partout. Pas une famille d'Europe que je ne connaisse. — J'entends des familles comme la mienne, que tiennent tout de la déclaration des Droits de l'Homme. — J'ai connu chaque fils de famille!

Si j'avais des antécédents à un point quelconque de l'histoire de France!

Mais non, rien.

Il m'est bien évident que j'ai toujours été race inférieure. Je

Bad Blood

I get from my Gallic ancestors my pale blue eye, my small brain, and my awkwardness in fighting. I find my clothes as barbaric as theirs. But I do not butter my hair.

The Gauls were the most inept flayers of beasts and scorchers of grass of their time.

From them, I get: idolatry and the love of sacrilege; — oh! all the vices, wrath, lust, — magnificent, the lust; — above all, falsehood and sloth.

I abhor all trades. Masters and workers, all peasants, ignoble. The hand with the pen is worth the hand with the plow. — What an age of hands! — I shall never have my hand. Then, servility drives one too far. The honesty of beggars rends my heart. Criminals disgust like castrates: as for me, I am untouched, and it is all the same to me.

But! who made my tongue so treacherous, that it has till now guided and safeguarded my slothfulness? Without employing even my body to earn my living, and more idle than the toad, I have lived everywhere. Not a family in Europe that I do not know. — I mean families like my own, that owe all to the declaration of the Rights of Man. — I have known every youth of good birth!

If only I had antecedents at any point whatsoever in the history of France!

But no, nothing.

It is quite evident to me that I have always been of an in-

ne puis comprendre la révolte. Ma race ne se souleva jamais que pour piller: tels les loups à la bête qu'ils n'ont pas tuée.

Je me rappelle l'histoire de la France fille aînée de l'Église. J'aurais fait, manant, le voyage de terre sainte; j'ai dans la tête des routes dans les plaines souabes, des vues de Byzance, des remparts de Solyme; le culte de Marie, l'attendrissement sur le crucifié s'éveillent en moi parmi mille féeries profanes. — Je suis assis, lépreux, sur les pots cassés et les orties, au pied d'un mur rongé par le soleil. — Plus tard, reître, j'aurais bivaqué sous les nuits d'Allemagne.

Ah! encore: je danse le sabbat dans une rouge clairière, avec des vieilles et des enfants.

Je ne me souviens pas plus loin que cette terre-ci et le christianisme. Je n'en finirais pas de me revoir dans ce passé. Mais toujours seul; sans famille; même, quelle langue parlais-je? Je ne me vois jamais dans les conseils du Christ; ni dans les conseils des Seigneurs, — représentants du Christ.

Qu'étais-je au siècle dernier: je ne me retrouve qu'aujourd'hui. Plus de vagabonds, plus de guerres vagues. La race inférieure a tout couvert — le peuple, comme on dit, la raison; la nation et la science.

Oh! la science! On a tout repris. Pour le corps et pour l'âme, — le viatique, — on a la médecine et la philosophie, — les remèdes de bonnes femmes et les chansons populaires arrangées. Et les divertissements des princes et les jeux qu'ils interdisaient! Géographie, cosmographie, mécanique, chimie! . . .

La science, la nouvelle noblesse! Le progrès. Le monde marche! Pourquoi ne tournerait-il pas?

C'est la vision des nombres. Nous allons à l'*Esprit*. C'est

ferior race. I cannot understand revolt. My race never rose in rebellion except to plunder: like wolves with the beast they have not killed.

I recall the history of France, eldest daughter of the Church. As a villein, I would have made the pilgrimage to the Holy Land; I have in my head roads in the Swabian plains, views of Byzantium, ramparts of Jerusalem; the worship of Mary, compassion for the Crucified One awaken in me among a thousand profane enchantments. — I am seated, a leper, on the potsherds and the nettles, at the foot of a wall corroded by the sun. — Later, as a mercenary, I would have bivouacked under the nights of Germany.

Ah! once more: I dance the witches' sabbath in a red glade, with old women and children.

I don't remember farther back than this land and Christianity. I'd never cease seeing myself again in this past. But always alone; without family; also, what language did I speak? I never see myself in the councils of Christ; nor in the councils of the Lords, — representatives of Christ.

What was I in the last century: I do not find myself again in any time other than the present. No more vagabonds, no more vague wars. The inferior race has overrun everything — the masses, as we say, reason; the nation and science.

Oh! science! Everything has been revised. For the body and for the soul, — the viaticum, — we have medicine and philosophy, — old wives' remedies and arrangements of popular songs. And the diversions of princes and the games they prohibited! Geography, cosmography, mechanics, chemistry! . . .

Science, the new nobility! Progress. The world marches on! Why should it not turn round?

It's the vision of numbers. We're approaching the *Spirit*. What I say is quite certain, it's an oracle. I understand, and

47

très-certain, c'est oracle, ce que je dis. Je comprends, et ne sachant m'expliquer sans paroles païennes, je voudrais me taire.

Le sang païen revient! L'Esprit est proche, pourquoi Christ ne m'aide-t-il pas, en donnant à mon âme noblesse et liberté. Hélas! l'Évangile a passé! l'Évangile! l'Évangile.

J'attends Dieu avec gourmandise. Je suis de race inférieure de toute éternité.

Me voici sur la plage armoricaine. Que les villes s'allument dans le soir. Ma journée est faite; je quitte l'Europe. L'air marin brûlera mes poumons; les climats perdus me tanneront. Nager, broyer l'herbe, chasser, fumer surtout; boire des liqueurs fortes comme du métal bouillant, — comme faisaient ces chers ancêtres autour des feux.

Je reviendrai, avec des membres de fer, la peau sombre, l'œil furieux: sur mon masque, on me jugera d'une race forte. J'aurai de l'or: je serai oisif et brutal. Les femmes soignent ces féroces infirmes retour des pays chauds. Je serai mêlé aux affaires politiques. Sauvé.

Maintenant je suis maudit, j'ai horreur de la patrie. Le meilleur, c'est un sommeil bien ivre, sur la grève.

On ne part pas. — Reprenons les chemins d'ici, chargé de mon vice, le vice qui a poussé ses racines de souffrance à mon côté, dès l'âge de raison — qui monte au ciel, me bat, me renverse, me traîne.

not knowing how to explain myself without pagan words, I would choose to be silent.

The pagan blood returns! The Spirit is near; why doesn't Christ help me, by giving my soul nobility and freedom. Alas! the Gospel has passed by! the Gospel! the Gospel.

I await God ravenously. I am of a race inferior for all eternity.

Here I am on the Breton shore. Let the towns sparkle in the evening. My day is done; I am leaving Europe. The sea air will scorch my lungs; odd climates will tan me. To swim, to trample the grass, to hunt, above all, to smoke; to drink liquors strong as boiling metal, — as my dear ancestors did around their fires.

I shall come back, with limbs of iron, my skin dark, my eye furious: from my mask, people will judge me a member of a powerful race. I shall have gold: I shall be idle and brutal. Women take care of these ferocious invalids on their return from torrid countries. I shall be involved in political affairs. Saved.

At present I am cursed. I abhor my fatherland. The best thing of all is a very drunken sleep, on the beach.

One does not run away. — Let me again take to the roads of this place, burdened with my vice, the vice that has driven its roots of suffering into my side, from the years of discretion — the vice that rises to heaven, beats me, throws me down, drags me along.

La dernière innocence et la dernière timidité. C'est dit. Ne pas porter au monde mes dégoûts et mes trahisons.

Allons! La marche, le fardeau, le désert, l'ennui et la colère. A qui me louer? Quelle bête faut-il adorer? Quelle sainte image attaque-t-on? Quels cœurs briserai-je? Quel mensonge dois-je tenir? — Dans quel sang marcher?

Plutôt, se garder de la justice. — La vie dure, l'abrutissement simple, — soulever, le poing desséché, le couvercle du cercueil, s'asseoir, s'étouffer. Ainsi point de vieillesse, ni de dangers: la terreur n'est pas française.

— Ah! je suis tellement délaissé que j'offre à n'importe quelle divine image des élans vers la perfection.

O mon abnégation, ô ma charité merveilleuse! ici-bas, pourtant!

De profundis Domine, suis-je bête!

Encore tout enfant, j'admirais le forçat intraitable sur qui se referme toujours le bagne; je visitais les auberges et les garnis qu'il aurait sacrés par son séjour; je voyais *avec son idée* le ciel bleu et le travail fleuri de la campagne; je flairais sa fatalité dans les villes. Il avait plus de force qu'un saint, plus de bon sens qu'un voyageur — et lui, lui seul! pour témoin de sa gloire et de sa raison.

Sur les routes, par des nuits d'hiver, sans gîte, sans habits, sans pain, une voix étreignait mon cœur gelé: « Faiblessse ou force: te voilà, c'est la force. Tu ne sais ni où tu vas ni pourquoi tu vas, entre partout, réponds à tout. On ne te tuera pas

The last shred of innocence and the last vestige of shyness. I have spoken. Don't convey to the world my loathings and my betrayals.

Let's move on! The march, the burden, the desert, the boredom and the wrath.

To whom hire myself out? Which beast must be worshiped? What sacred image is being attacked? What hearts shall I shatter? What falsehood must I maintain? — In what blood wade?

Rather, guard against the law. — The hard life, plain brutishness, — to lift, with the shriveled fist, the lid of the coffin, to sit down in it, to suffocate. In this manner no old age, nor any dangers: terror is not French.

— Ah! I am so forsaken that I offer to any divine image whatsoever my drives toward perfection.

O my abnegation, O my marvelous charity! here on earth, however!

De profundis Domine, am I a fool!

When still quite a child, I admired the incorrigible convict on whom the prison gates always close again; I visited the inns and lodgings which he would have consecrated by his sojourn there; I saw *with his fancy* the blue sky and the flowery labor of the countryside; I scented his fatality in the towns. He had more fortitude than a saint, more common sense than a traveler — and he, he alone! served as witness to his glory and his reason.

On the roads, through winter nights, without shelter, without clothing, without bread, a voice would grip my frozen heart: "Weakness or strength: there you are, it is strength. You know neither where you are going nor why you are going;

plus que si tu étais cadavre. » Au matin j'avais le regard si
perdu et la contenance si morte, que ceux que j'ai rencontrés
~~ne m'ont peut-être pas vu.~~

Dans les villes la boue m'apparaissait soudainement rouge
et noire, comme une glace quand la lampe circule dans la
chambre voisine, comme un trésor dans la forêt! Bonne
chance, criais-je, et je voyais une mer de flammes et de fumée
au ciel; et, à gauche, à droite, toutes les richesses flambant
comme un milliard de tonnerres.

Mais l'orgie et la camaraderie des femmes m'étaient inter-
dites. Pas même un compagnon. Je me voyais devant une foule
exaspérée, en face du peloton d'exécution, pleurant du malheur
qu'ils n'aient pu comprendre, et pardonnant! — Comme
Jeanne d'Arc! — « Prêtres, professeurs, maîtres, vous vous
trompez en me livrant à la justice. Je n'ai jamais été de ce
peuple-ci; je n'ai jamais été chrétien; je suis de la race qui
chantait dans le supplice; je ne comprends pas les lois; je n'ai
pas le sens moral, je suis une brute: vous vous trompez . . . »

Oui, j'ai les yeux fermés à votre lumière. Je suis une bête,
un nègre. Mais je puis être sauvé. Vous êtes de faux nègres,
vous maniaques, féroces, avares. Marchand, tu es nègre;
magistrat, tu es nègre; général, tu es nègre; empereur, vieille
démangeaison, tu es nègre: tu as bu d'une liqueur non taxée,
de la fabrique de Satan. — Ce peuple est inspiré par la fièvre
et le cancer. Infirmes et vieillards sont tellement respectables
qu'ils demandent à être bouillis. — Le plus malin est de quitter
ce continent, où la folie rôde pour pourvoir d'otages ces misérables. J'entre au vrai royaume des enfants de Cham.

Connais-je encore la nature? me connais-je? — *Plus de mots.*
J'ensevelis les morts dans mon ventre. Cris, tambour, danse,
danse, danse, danse! Je ne vois même pas l'heure où, les blancs
débarquant, je tomberai au néant.

enter everywhere, respond to everything. No one will kill you any more than if you were a corpse." In the morning I'd have such a lost look and such a dead countenance, that those whom I encountered *possibly did not see me*.

In the towns the mud suddenly seemed to me red and black, like a mirror when the lamp moves around in the adjoining room, like a treasure in the forest! Good luck, I cried out, and I saw a sea of flames and smoke in the sky; and, on the left, on the right, all the riches blazing like a billion thunderbolts.

But orgy and the intimacy of women were forbidden me. Not even a male companion. I saw myself before an enraged mob, facing the firing squad, weeping with the misery which they could not have understood, and forgiving them! — Like Joan of Arc! — "Priests, professors, masters, you are making a mistake in delivering me to justice. I have never been of this people; I have never been Christian; I am of the race which used to sing under torture; I do not understand the laws; I do not have the moral sense, I am a brute: you are making a mistake . . ."

Yes, my eyes are closed to your light. I am a beast, a Negro. But I can be saved. You are false Negroes, you maniacs, fierce, miserly. Merchant, you're a Negro; magistrate, you're a Negro; general, you're a Negro; emperor, old mangy itch, you're a Negro: you have drunk untaxed liquor, from Satan's distillery. — This people is inspired by fever and cancer. Invalids and old men are so respectable that they beg to be boiled. — The shrewdest thing is to abandon this continent, where madness prowls to provide these wretches with hostages. I am entering the true kingdom of the children of Ham.

Do I know nature yet? do I know myself? — *No more words.* I bury the dead in my belly. Cries, drum, dance, dance, dance, dance! I do not even see the time when, with the whites disembarking, I shall sink into nothingness.

Faim, soif, cris, danse, danse, danse, danse!

Les blancs débarquent. Le canon! Il faut se soumettre au baptême, s'habiller, travailler.

J'ai reçu au cœur le coup de grâce. Ah! je ne l'avais pas prévu!

Je n'ai point fait le mal. Les jours vont m'être légers, le repentir me sera épargné. Je n'aurai pas eu les tourments de l'âme presque morte au bien, où remonte la lumière sévère comme les cierges funéraires. Le sort du fils de famille, cercueil prématuré couvert de limpides larmes. Sans doute la débauche est bête, le vice est bête; il faut jeter la pourriture à l'écart. Mais l'horloge ne sera pas arrivée à ne plus sonner que l'heure de la pure douleur! Vais-je être enlevé comme un enfant, pour jouer au paradis dans l'oubli de tout le malheur!

Vite! est-il d'autres vies? — Le sommeil dans la richesse est impossible. La richesse a toujours été bien public. L'amour divin seul octroie les clefs de la science. Je vois que la nature n'est qu'un spectacle de bonté. Adieu chimères, idéals, erreurs.

Le chant raisonnable des anges s'élève du navire sauveur: c'est l'amour divin. — Deux amours! je puis mourir de l'amour terrestre, mourir de dévouement. J'ai laissé des âmes dont la peine s'accroîtra de mon départ! Vous me choisissez parmi les naufragés; ceux qui restent sont-ils pas mes amis?

Sauvez-les!

La raison m'est née. Le monde est bon. Je bénirai la vie. J'aimerai mes frères. Ce ne sont plus des promesses d'enfance. Ni l'espoir d'échapper à la vieillesse et à la mort. Dieu fait ma force, et je loue Dieu.

Hunger, thirst, cries, dance, dance, dance, dance!

The whites disembark. The cannon! It is necessary to submit to baptism, to wear clothes, to toil.

I have received in my heart the coup de grâce. Ah! I had not foreseen it!

I have done no evil. My days will be lighthearted, I shall be spared repentance. I shall not have had the torments of the soul almost dead to righteousness, in which the light rises as sober as funeral candles. The lot of a young man of good family, a premature coffin covered with limpid tears. Without doubt debauchery is stupid, vice is stupid; it is necessary to cast aside corruption. But the clock will not have come to sound only the hour of pure sorrow! Am I going to be carried off like a child, to play in paradise oblivious of all misfortune!

Quickly! are there other lives? — In wealth, sleep is impossible. Wealth has always been public property. Divine love alone confers the keys of knowledge. I see that nature is nothing but a spectacle of goodness. Farewell chimeras, ideals, errors.

The reasonable song of angels rises from the savior ship: it is the love divine. — Two loves! I can die of earthly love, I can die of devotion. I have left behind souls whose pain will increase at my departure! You are choosing me from among the shipwrecked; those who remain, aren't they my friends?

Save them!

Reason is born within me. The world is good. I shall bless life. I shall love my brothers. These are no longer childhood promises. Nor the hope of escaping old age and death. God gives my strength, and I extol God.

L'ennui n'est plus mon amour. Les rages, les débauches, la folie, dont je sais tous les élans et les désastres, — tout mon fardeau est déposé. Apprécions sans vertige l'étendue de mon innocence.

Je ne serais plus capable de demander le réconfort d'une bastonnade. Je ne me crois pas embarqué pour une noce avec Jésus-Christ pour beau-père.

Je ne suis pas prisonnier de ma raison. J'ai dit: Dieu. Je veux la liberté dans le salut: comment la poursuivre? Les goûts frivoles m'ont quitté. Plus besoin de dévouement ni d'amour divin. Je ne regrette pas le siècle des cœurs sensibles. Chacun a sa raison, mépris et charité: je retiens ma place au sommet de cette angélique échelle de bon sens.

Quant au bonheur établi, domestique ou non . . . non, je ne peux pas. Je suis trop dissipé, trop faible. La vie fleurit par le travail, vieille vérité: moi, ma vie n'est pas assez pesante, elle s'envole et flotte loin au-dessus de l'action, ce cher point du monde.

Comme je deviens vieille fille, à manquer du courage d'aimer la mort!

Si Dieu m'accordait le calme céleste, aérien, la prière, — comme les anciens saints. — les saints! des forts! les anachorètes, des artistes comme il n'en faut plus!

Farce continuelle! Mon innocence me ferait pleurer. La vie est la farce à mener par tous.

Boredom is no longer my love. Rages, debaucheries, madness, all of whose transports and disasters I know, — my whole burden is set down. Let's appreciate without giddiness the extent of my innocence.

I would no longer be capable of requesting the comfort of a bastinado. I do not believe I have embarked on a wedding with Jesus Christ as my father-in-law.

I am not a prisoner of my reason. I have said: God. I wish for freedom in salvation: how to pursue it? Frivolous tastes have left me. No more need for devotion nor for divine love. I do not miss the age of sensitive hearts. Everyone has his reason, scorn and charity: I retain my place at the top of this angelic ladder of common sense.

As for established happiness, domestic or not . . . no, I cannot. I am too dissipated, too weak. Life flowers through toil, an old truth: as for me, my life is not sufficiently weighty, it takes wing and floats far above the action, that cherished focus of the world.

What an old maid I'm becoming, to lack the courage to love death!

If only God would accord me heavenly, ethereal calmness, prayer, — like the ancient saints — the saints! powerful men! the anchorites, artists such as are no longer needed!

An endless farce! My innocence would make me weep. Life is the farce all have to perform.

Assez! Voici la punition. — *En marche!*

Ah! les poumons brûlent, les tempes grondent! la nuit roule dans mes yeux, par ce soleil! le cœur . . . les membres. . .

Où va-t-on? au combat? Je suis faible! les autres avancent. Les outils, les armes . . . le temps! . . .

Feu! feu sur moi! Là! ou je me rends. — Lâches!

— Je me tue! Je me jette aux pieds des chevaux!

Ah! . . .

— Je m'y habituerai.

Ce serait la vie française, le sentier de l'honneur!

Enough! This is the punishment. — *On the march!*

Ah! my lungs burn, my temples grumble! night revolves in my eyes, through this sunshine! my heart . . . my limbs . . .

Where are we going? into combat? I am weak! the others advance. The tools, the weapons . . . the hour! . . .

Fire! fire on me! There! or I surrender. — Cowards!

— I kill myself! I fling myself under the horses' hoofs! Ah! . . .

— I'll get used to it.

That would be the French way of life, the path of honor!

Nuit de l'enfer

J'ai avalé une fameuse gorgée de poison. — Trois fois béni soit le conseil qui m'est arrivé! — Les entrailles me brûlent. La violence du venin tord mes membres, me rend difforme, me terrasse. Je meurs de soif, j'étouffe, je ne puis crier. C'est l'enfer, l'éternelle peine! Voyez comme le feu se relève! Je brûle comme il faut. Va, démon!

J'avais entrevu la conversion au bien et au bonheur, le salut. Puis-je décrire la vision, l'air de l'enfer ne souffre pas les hymnes! C'était des millions de créatures charmantes, un suave concert spirituel, la force et la paix, les nobles ambitions, que sais-je?

Les nobles ambitions!

Et c'est encore la vie! — Si la damnation est éternelle! Un homme qui veut se mutiler est bien damné, n'est-ce pas? Je me crois en enfer, donc j'y suis. C'est l'exécution du catéchisme. Je suis esclave de mon baptême. Parents, vous avez fait mon malheur et vous avez fait le vôtre. Pauvre innocent! — L'enfer ne peut attaquer les païens. — C'est la vie encore! Plus tard, les délices de la damnation seront plus profondes. Un crime, vite, que je tombe au néant, de par la loi humaine.

Tais-toi, mais tais-toi! . . . C'est la honte, le reproche, ici: Satan qui dit que le feu est ignoble, que ma colère est affreusement sotte. — Assez! . . . Des erreurs qu'on me souffle, magies, parfums faux, musiques puériles. — Et dire que je tiens la vérité, que je vois la justice: j'ai un jugement sain et arrêté, je suis prêt pour la perfection. . . Orgueil. — La peau de ma tête se dessèche. Pitié! Seigneur, j'ai peur. J'ai soif, si

Night of Hell

I have swallowed a first-rate draught of poison. — Thrice blessed be the counsel that came to me! — My entrails are on fire. The violence of the venom wrings my limbs, deforms me, fells me. I am dying of thirst, I am suffocating, I cannot cry out. This is hell, the everlasting punishment! Mark how the fire surges up again! I am burning properly. There you are, demon!

I had caught a glimpse of conversion to righteousness and happiness, salvation. May I describe the vision; the atmosphere of hell does not permit hymns! It consisted of millions of charming creatures, a sweet sacred concert, power and peace, noble ambitions, and goodness knows what else.

Noble ambitions!

And yet this is life! — What if damnation is eternal! A man who chooses to mutilate himself is rightly damned, isn't he? I believe that I am in hell, consequently I am there. This is the effect of the catechism. I am the slave of my baptism. Parents, you have caused my affliction and you have caused your own. Poor innocent! — Hell cannot assail pagans. — This is life, nevertheless! Later, the delights of damnation will be deeper. A crime, quickly, that I may sink to nothingness, in accordance with human law.

Be silent, do be silent! . . . There is shame, reproof, in this place: Satan who says that the fire is disgraceful, that my wrath is frightfully foolish. — Enough! . . . The errors that are whispered to me, enchantments, false perfumes, childish melodies. — And to say that I possess truth, that I understand justice: I have a sound and steady judgment, I am prepared for perfection . . . Pride. — The skin of my head is drying

soif! Ah! l'enfance, l'herbe, la pluie, le lac sur les pierres, *le clair de lune quand le clocher sonnait douze* . . . le diable est au clocher, à cette heure. Marie! Sainte Vierge! . . . — Horreur de ma bêtise.

Là-bas, ne sont-ce pas des âmes honnêtes, qui me veulent du bien? . . . Venez. . . J'ai un oreiller sur la bouche, elles ne m'entendent pas, ce sont des fantômes. Puis, jamais personne ne pense à autrui. Qu'on n'approche pas. Je sens le roussi, c'est certain.

Les hallucinations sont innombrables. C'est bien ce que j'ai toujours eu: plus de foi en l'histoire, l'oubli des principes. Je m'en tairai: poëtes et visionnaires seraient jaloux. Je suis mille fois le plus riche, soyons avare comme la mer.

Ah ça! l'horloge de la vie s'est arrêtée tout à l'heure. Je ne suis plus au monde. — La théologie est sérieuse, l'enfer est certainement *en bas* — et le ciel en haut. — Extase, cauchemar, sommeil dans un nid de flammes.

Que de malices dans l'attention dans la campagne. . . Satan, Ferdinand, court avec les graines sauvages. . . Jésus marche sur les ronces purpurines, sans les courber. . . Jésus marchait sur les eaux irritées. La lanterne nous le montra debout, blanc et des tresses brunes, au flanc d'une vague d'émeraude. . .

Je vais dévoiler tous les mystères: mystères religieux ou naturels, mort, naissance, avenir, passé, cosmogonie, néant. Je suis maître en fantasmagories.

Écoutez! . . .

J'ai tous les talents! — Il n'y a personne ici et il y a quelqu'un: je ne voudrais pas répandre mon trésor. — Veut-on des chants nègres, des danses de houris? Veut-on que je disparaisse, que je plonge à la recherche de l'*anneau*? Veut-on? Je ferai de l'or, des remèdes.

up. Pity! Lord, I am terrified. I am thirsty, so thirsty! Ah! childhood, the grass, the rain, the lake upon the stones, *the moonlight when the bell tower was striking twelve* . . . the devil is in the bell tower, at that hour. Mary! Blessed Virgin! . . . — The horror of my stupidity.

Over there, are they not honest souls, who wish me well? . . . Come . . . I have a pillow over my mouth, they don't hear me, they are phantoms. Besides, no one ever thinks of others. Let no one approach. I reek of burning, that's certain.

The hallucinations are countless. It's exactly what I've always had: no more faith in history, neglect of principles. I shall be silent about this: poets and visionaries would be jealous. I am a thousand times the richest, let us be avaricious like the sea.

Now then! the clock of life has just stopped. I am no longer in the world. — Theology is serious, hell is certainly *below* — and heaven above. — Ecstasy, nightmare, sleep in a nest of flames.

What pranks during my vigilance in the country . . . Satan, Ferdinand, races with the wild seeds . . . Jesus walks on the purplish briers, without bending them . . . Jesus used to walk on the troubled waters. The lantern revealed him to us, a figure standing, pale and with brown tresses, beside a wave of emerald. . .

I am going to unveil all the mysteries: mysteries religious or natural, death, birth, futurity, antiquity, cosmogony, nothingness. I am a master of phantasmagories.

Listen! . . .

I have all the talents! — There is nobody here and there is somebody: I would not wish to scatter my treasure. — Do you wish for Negro chants, dances of houris? Do you wish me to vanish, to dive in search of the *ring*? Do you? I shall produce gold, cures.

Fiez-vous donc à moi, la foi soulage, guide, guérit. Tous, venez, — même les petits enfants, — que je vous console, qu'on répande pour vous son cœur, — le cœur merveilleux! — Pauvres hommes, travailleurs! Je ne demande pas de prières; avec votre confiance seulement, je serai heureux.

— Et pensons à moi. Ceci me fait peu regretter le monde. J'ai de la chance de ne pas souffrir plus. Ma vie ne fut que folies douces, c'est regrettable.

Bah! faisons toutes les grimaces imaginables.

Décidément, nous sommes hors du monde. Plus aucun son. Mon tact a disparu. Ah! mon château, ma Saxe, mon bois de saules. Les soirs, les matins, les nuits, les jours. . . Suis-je las!

Je devrais avoir mon enfer pour la colère, mon enfer pour l'orgueil, — et l'enfer de la caresse; un concert d'enfers.

Je meurs de lassitude. C'est le tombeau, je m'en vais aux vers, horreur de l'horreur! Satan, farceur, tu veux me dissoudre, avec tes charmes. Je réclame. Je réclame! un coup de fourche, une goutte de feu.

Ah! remonter à la vie! Jeter les yeux sur nos difformités. Et ce poison, ce baiser mille fois maudit! Ma faiblesse, la cruauté du monde! Mon Dieu, pitié, cachez-moi, je me tiens trop mal! — Je suis caché et je ne le suis pas.

C'est le feu qui se relève avec son damné.

Rely, then, upon me: faith comforts, guides, heals. All of you, come, — even the little children, — that I may console you, that one may pour out his heart for you, — the marvelous heart! — Poor men, laborers! I do not ask for prayers; with your confidence alone, I shall be happy.

— And let's think of me. This makes me miss the world very little. I have the good fortune not to suffer any longer. My life was nothing but sweet follies, regrettably.

Bah! let's make all the grimaces imaginable.

Decidedly, we are out of the world. No more sound. My sense of touch has disappeared. Ah! my castle, my Saxony, my forest of willows. The evenings, the mornings, the nights, the days . . . Am I weary!

I ought to have my hell for wrath, my hell for pride, — and the hell of the caress; a concert of hells.

I am dying of weariness. This is the tomb, I am going to the worms, horror of horrors! Satan, jester, you wish to undo me, with your spells. I protest. I protest! one jab of the pitchfork, one lick of fire.

Ah! to rise again to life! To cast eyes upon our deformities. And that poison, that kiss a thousand times accursed! My weakness, the cruelty of the world! Dear God, your mercy, hide me, I regard myself too poorly! — I am hidden and I am not.

It is the fire that rises again with the soul condemned to it.

Délires

I

Écoutons la confession d'un compagnon d'enfer:

« O divin Époux, mon Seigneur, ne refusez pas la confession de la plus triste de vos servantes. Je suis perdue. Je suis soûle. Je suis impure. Quelle vie!

« Pardon, divin Seigneur, pardon! Ah! pardon! Que de larmes! Et que de larmes encore plus tard, j'espère!

« Plus tard, je connaîtrai le divin Époux! Je suis née soumise à Lui. — L'autre peut me battre maintenant!

« A présent, je suis au fond du monde! O mes amies! . . . non, pas mes amies . . . Jamais délires ni tortures semblables . . . Est-ce bête!

« Ah! je souffre, je crie. Je souffre vraiment. Tout pourtant m'est permis, chargée du mépris des plus méprisables cœurs.

« Enfin, faisons cette confidence, quitte à la répéter vingt autres fois, — aussi morne, aussi insignifiante!

« Je suis esclave de l'Époux infernal, celui qui a perdu les vierges folles. C'est bien ce démon-là. Ce n'est pas un spectre, ce n'est pas un fantôme. Mais moi qui ai perdu la sagesse, qui suis damnée et morte au monde, — on ne me tuera pas! — Comment vous le décrire! Je ne sais même plus parler. Je suis en deuil, je pleure, j'ai peur. Un peu de fraîcheur, Seigneur, si vous voulez, si vous voulez bien!

Deliriums

I

FOOLISH VIRGIN
THE INFERNAL BRIDEGROOM

Let us listen to the confession of a companion in hell:

"O divine Bridegroom, my Lord, do not refuse the confession of the saddest of your maidservants. I am lost. I am intoxicated. I am impure. What a life!

"Forgiveness, divine Lord, forgiveness! Ah! forgiveness! How many tears! And how many tears again later, I trust!

"Later, I shall know the divine Bridegroom! I was born submissive to Him. — The other one can thrash me now!

"At present, I am at the bottom of the world! O my friends! . . . no, not my friends . . . Never deliriums or tortures like these . . . How senseless it is!

"Ah! I suffer, I cry out. I really do suffer. Everything, however, is permitted me, charged with the contempt of the most contemptible hearts.

"Finally, let us make this disclosure, even if we have to repeat it twenty times over, — as dismal and as insignificant as it is!

"I am the slave of the infernal Bridegroom, he who ruined the foolish virgins. He is surely that very demon. He is not a specter, he is not a phantom. But I who have lost my discretion, who am damned and dead to the world, — no one will kill me! — How am I to portray him for you! I do not even know how to speak anymore. I am in mourning, I weep, I am terrified. A little coolness, Lord, if you are willing, if you are truly willing!

« Je suis veuve . . . — J'étais veuve . . . — mais oui, j'ai été bien sérieuse jadis, et je ne suis pas née pour devenir squelette! . . . — Lui était presque un enfant . . . Ses délicatesses mystérieuses m'avaient séduite. J'ai oublié tout mon devoir humain pour le suivre. Quelle vie! La vraie vie est absente. Nous ne sommes pas au monde. Je vais où il va, il le faut. Et souvent il s'emporte contre moi, *moi, la pauvre âme*. Le Démon! — C'est un Démon, vous savez, *ce n'est pas un homme*.

« Il dit: « Je n'aime pas les femmes. L'amour est à réinventer, on le sait. Elles ne peuvent plus que vouloir une position assurée. La position gagnée, cœur et beauté sont mis de côté: il ne reste que froid dédain, l'aliment du mariage, aujourd'hui. Ou bien je vois des femmes, avec les signes du bonheur, dont, moi, j'aurai pu faire de bonnes camarades, dévorées tout d'abord par des brutes sensibles comme des bûchers . . . »

« Je l'écoute faisant de l'infamie une gloire, de la cruauté un charme. « Je suis de race lointaine: mes pères étaient Scandinaves: ils se perçaient les côtes, buvaient leur sang. — Je me ferai des entailles par tout le corps, je me tatouerai, je veux devenir hideux comme un Mongol: tu verras, je hurlerai dans les rues. Je veux devenir bien fou de rage. Ne me montre jamais de bijoux, je ramperais et me tordrais sur le tapis. Ma richesse, je la voudrais tachée de sang partout. Jamais je ne travaillerai . . . » Plusieurs nuits, son démon me saisissant, nous nous roulions, je luttais avec lui! — Les nuits, souvent, ivre, il se poste dans des rues ou dans des maisons, pour m'épouvanter mortellement. — « On me coupera vraiment le cou; ce sera « dégoûtant. » Oh! ces jours où il veut marcher avec l'air du crime!

« Parfois il parle, en une façon de patois attendri, de la mort qui fait repentir, des malheureux qui existent certainement,

"I am a widow . . . — I was a widow . . . — why yes, I was quite serious once, and I was not born to become a skeleton! . . . — He was practically a child . . . His mysterious delicate ways had seduced me. I forgot my every human obligation in order to follow him. What a life! Real life is absent. We are not in the world. I go where he goes, I must. And often he loses his temper with me, *me, the poor soul*. The Demon! — He is a Demon, you know; *he is not a man*.

"He says: 'I don't like women. Love has to be invented over again, that's known. They can do no more than wish for a secure position. When the position has been gained, love and beauty are put aside: nothing remains except frigid disdain, the sustenance of marriage, nowadays. Or else I see women, with the signs of happiness, of whom I could have made good companions, utterly consumed from the outset by brutes as sensitive as funeral piles . . .'

"I listen to him turning infamy into glory, cruelty into charm. 'I am of a far-off people: my ancestors were Scandinavians: they pierced their sides, drank their own blood. — I will make gashes over my entire body, I will tattoo myself, I wish to become as hideous as a Mongol: you will see, I will howl in the streets. I wish to become quite mad with rage. Never show me jewels, I would crawl and writhe on the carpet. My riches, I would like them stained with blood all over. Never will I work . . .' On some nights, his demon seizing me, we tumbled about, I wrestled with him! — Often, at night, drunk, he takes up his position in the streets or houses, in order to terrify me to death. — 'Someone will really behead me; it will be "disgusting." ' Oh! those days when he is determined to walk about with an air of crime!

"Every now and then he speaks, in a kind of tender patois, about death that brings repentance, about the unfortunates

des travaux pénibles, des départs qui déchirent les cœurs. Dans les bouges où nous nous enivrions, il pleurait en considérant ceux qui nous entouraient, bétail de la misère. Il relevait les ivrognes dans les rues noires. Il avait la pitié d'une mère méchante pour les petits enfants. — Il s'en allait avec des gentillesses de petite fille au catéchisme. — Il feignait d'être éclairé sur tout, commerce, art, médecine. — Je le suivais, il le faut!

« Je voyais tout le décor dont, en esprit, il s'entourait: vêtements, draps, meubles; je lui prêtais des armes, une autre figure. Je voyais tout ce qui le touchait, comme il aurait voulu le créer pour lui. Quand il me semblait avoir l'esprit inerte, je le suivais, moi, dans des actions étranges et compliquées, loin, bonnes ou mauvaises: j'étais sûre de ne jamais entrer dans son monde. A côté de son cher corps endormi, que d'heures des nuits j'ai veillé, cherchant pourquoi il voulait tant s'évader de la réalité. Jamais homme n'eut pareil vœu. Je reconnaissais, — sans craindre pour lui, — qu'il pouvait être un sérieux danger dans la société. — Il a peut-être des secrets pour *changer la vie?* Non, il ne fait qu'en chercher, me répliquais-je. Enfin sa charité est ensorcelée, et j'en suis la prisonnière. Aucune autre âme n'aurait assez de force, — force de désespoir! — pour la supporter, — pour être protégée et aimée par lui. D'ailleurs, je ne me le figurais pas avec une autre âme: on voit son Ange, jamais l'Ange d'un autre, — je crois. J'étais dans son âme comme dans un palais qu'on a vidé pour ne pas voir une personne si peu noble que vous: voilà tout. Hélas! je dépendais bien de lui. Mais que voulait-il avec mon existence terne et lâche? Il ne me rendait pas meilleure, s'il ne me faisait pas mourir! Tristement

who certainly do exist, about painful toil, about separations that rend hearts. In the hovels where we would get drunk, he would weep while contemplating those who surrounded us, cattle of misery. He would raise drunkards to their feet in the dark streets. He felt the pity of a wayward mother for little children. — He would go away with the graciousness of a little girl on her way to catechism. — He pretended to be enlightened about everything, commerce, art, medicine. — I followed him, of necessity!

"I would see the whole setting with which, in his fancy, he surrounded himself: clothes, sheets, furniture; I lent him weapons, another guise. I saw everything which concerned him, as he would have wished to create it for himself. When he seemed to me to be apathetic, I would follow him, far, myself, in strange and complicated actions, good or bad: I was sure of never entering his world. Beside his dear sleeping body, how many hours of the nights have I kept watch, seeking the reason why he wished so much to escape from reality. Never did a man have a wish equal to it. I recognized, — without being apprehensive for him, — that he could be a serious danger in society. — Does he perhaps possess secrets for *transforming life?* No, he is doing no more than searching for them, I would answer myself. In short, his charity is bewitched, and I am its prisoner. No other soul would have sufficient strength, — strength of despair! — to endure it, — to be protected and loved by him. Besides, I never imagined him with another soul: one sees his own Angel, never the Angel of another, — I think. I existed in his soul as in a palace which has been emptied so that no one should see a person so ignoble as you: that's all. Alas! I depended entirely on him. But what did he want with my dull and cowardly existence? He was not improving me, if he was not killing me! Sadly vexed, I said

dépitée, je lui dis quelquefois: « Je te comprends. » Il haussait les épaules.

« Ainsi, mon chagrin se renouvelant sans cesse, et me trouvant plus égarée à mes yeux, — comme à tous les yeux qui auraient voulu me fixer, si je n'eusse été condamnée pour jamais à l'oubli de tous! — j'avais de plus en plus faim de sa bonté. Avec ses baisers et ses étreintes amies, c'était bien un ciel, un sombre ciel où j'entrais, et où j'aurais voulu être laissée, pauvre, sourde, muette, aveugle. Déjà j'en prenais l'habitude. Je nous voyais comme deux bons enfants, libres de se promener dans le Paradis de tristesse. Nous nous accordions. Bien émus, nous travaillions ensemble. Mais, après une pénétrante caresse, il disait: « Comme ça te paraîtra drôle, quand je n'y serai plus, ce par quoi tu as passé. Quand tu n'auras plus mes bras sous ton cou, ni mon cœur pour t'y reposer, ni cette bouche sur tes yeux. Parce qu'il faudra que je m'en aille, très loin, un jour. Puis il faut que j'en aide d'autres: c'est mon devoir. Quoique ce ne soit guère ragoûtant . . . , chère âme . . . » Tout de suite je me pressentais, lui parti, en proie au vertige, précipitée dans l'ombre la plus affreuse: la mort. Je lui faisais promettre qu'il ne me lâcherait pas. Il l'a faite vingt fois, cette promesse d'amant. C'était aussi frivole que moi lui disant: « Je te comprends. »

« Ah! je n'ai jamais été jalouse de lui. Il ne me quittera pas, je crois. Que devenir? Il n'a pas une connaissance; il ne travaillera jamais. Il veut vivre somnambule. Seules, sa bonté et sa charité lui donneraient-elles droit dans le monde réel? Par instants, j'oublie la pitié où je suis tombée: lui me rendra forte, nous voyagerons, nous chasserons dans les déserts, nous dormirons sur les pavés des villes inconnues, sans soins, sans peines. Ou je me réveillerai, et les lois et les mœurs auront changé, —

to him sometimes: 'I understand you.' He would shrug his shoulders.

"Thus, my sorrow being unceasingly renewed, and finding myself more lost in my own eyes, — as in the eyes of all who would have wished to stare at me, if I had not been condemned forever to be forgotten by everyone! — I hungered more and more for his kindness. With his kisses and his fond embraces, it was certainly a heaven, an overcast heaven which I entered, and where I would have wished to be left, poor, deaf, dumb, blind. Already I was getting used to it. I regarded us as two good children, free to roam within the Paradise of sadness. We suited one another. Quite moved, we toiled together. But, after a poignant caress, he would say: 'How odd this will seem to you, when I am no longer here, this which you have gone through. When you no longer have my arms upon your neck, nor my heart to rest on, nor these lips on your eyes. Because I shall have to go away, very far, one day. Then I must help others: it is my duty. Though it will hardly be pleasing . . . , dear soul . . .' At once I could foresee myself, with him gone, in the clutch of vertigo, plunged into the most frightful darkness: death. I made him promise that he would not cast me off. He made it twenty times, this promise of a lover. It was as frivolous as my saying to him: 'I understand you.'

"Ah! I have never been jealous of him. He will not leave me, I think. What's to become of him? He hasn't one acquaintance; he will never work. He wants to live as a somnambulist. Would his goodness and his charity alone give him any claim in the real world? Off and on, I forget the pitiful state into which I have sunk: he will make me strong, we shall travel, we shall hunt in wildernesses, we shall sleep on the pavements of unknown towns, without cares, without troubles. Or I shall wake up, and laws and morals will have

grâce à son pouvoir magique, — le monde, en restant le même,
me laissera à mes désirs, joies, nonchalances. Oh! la vie
d'aventures qui existe dans les livres des enfants, pour me
récompenser, j'ai tant souffert, me la donneras-tu? Il ne peut
pas. J'ignore son idéal. Il m'a dit avoir des regrets, des espoirs:
cela ne doit pas me regarder. Parle-t-il à Dieu? Peut-être
devrais-je m'adresser à Dieu. Je suis au plus profond de l'abîme,
et je ne sais plus prier.

« S'il m'expliquait ses tristesses, les comprendrais-je plus que
ses railleries? Il m'attaque, il passe des heures à me faire honte
de tout ce qui m'a pu toucher au monde, et s'indigne si je
pleure.

« — Tu vois cet élégant jeune homme, entrant dans la belle
et calme maison: il s'appelle Duval, Dufour, Armand, Maurice,
que sais-je? Une femme s'est dévouée à aimer ce méchant idiot:
elle est morte, c'est certes une sainte au ciel, à présent. Tu me
feras mourir comme il a fait mourir cette femme. C'est notre
sort, à nous, cœurs charitables . . . » Hélas! il avait des jours
où tous les hommes agissant lui paraissaient les jouets de
délires grotesques; il riait affreusement, longtemps. — Puis, il
reprenait ses manières de jeune mère, de sœur aimée. S'il était
moins sauvage, nous serions sauvés! Mais sa douceur aussi est
mortelle. Je lui suis soumise. — Ah! je suis folle!

« Un jour peut-être il disparaîtra merveilleusement; mais il
faut que je sache, s'il doit remonter à un ciel, que je voie un
peu l'assomption de mon petit ami! »

Drôle de ménage!

changed, — thanks to his magic power, — the world, while remaining the same, will leave me to my desires, my joys, my nonchalant ways. Oh! the adventurous life that exists in children's books, will you give it to me to repay me, I have suffered so much? He cannot. I do not know his ideal. He has told me he has regrets, hopes: this is not likely to concern me. Does he speak to God? Perhaps I ought to appeal to God. I am at the very bottom of the abyss, and I no longer know how to pray.

"If he explained his sorrows to me, would I understand them better than his railleries? He attacks me, he spends hours making me ashamed of everything that has been able to move me in the world, and is indignant if I weep.

"— You see that elegant young man, entering the fine and serene house: his name is Duval, Dufour, Armand, Maurice, for all I know. A woman devoted herself to loving this worthless fool: she is dead, she is most certainly a saint in heaven, at present. You will kill me as he killed that woman. That is our lot, assigned to us, the loving hearts . . .' Alas! he had days when all active men seeemed to him the playthings of grotesque deliriums; he would laugh frightfully, for a long time. — Then, he would resume his demeanor of young mother, of beloved sister. If only he were less wild, we should be saved! But his sweetness also is deadly. I am submissive to him. — Ah! I am insane!

"One day perhaps he will disappear miraculously; but I must know if he is likely to rise to some heaven again, so that I may view briefly the assumption of my little lover!"

A strange ménage!

Délires
II
ALCHIMIE DU VERBE

À moi. L'histoire d'une de mes folies.

Depuis longtemps je me vantais de posséder tous les paysages possibles, et trouvais dérisoires les célébrités de la peinture et de la poésie moderne.

J'aimais les peintures idiotes, dessus de portes, décors, toiles de saltimbanques, enseignes, enluminures populaires; la littérature démodée, latin d'église, livres érotiques sans orthographe, romans de nos aïeules, contes de fées, petits livres de l'enfance, opéras vieux, refrains niais, rhythmes naïfs.

Je rêvais croisades, voyages de découvertes dont on n'a pas de relations, républiques sans histoires, guerres de religion étouffées, révolutions de mœurs, déplacements de races et de continents: je croyais à tous les enchantements.

J'inventai la couleur des voyelles! — A noir, E blanc, I rouge, O bleu, U vert. — Je réglai la forme et le mouvement de chaque consonne, et, avec des rhythmes instinctifs, je me flattai d'inventer un verbe poétique accessible, un jour ou l'autre, à tous les sens. Je réservais la traduction.

Ce fut d'abord une étude. J'écrivais des silences, des nuits, je notais l'inexprimable. Je fixais des vertiges.

> Loin des oiseaux, des troupeaux, des villageoises,
> Que buvais-je, à genoux dans cette bruyère
> Entourée de tendres bois de noisetiers,
> Dans un brouillard d'après-midi tiède et vert?

Deliriums
II
ALCHEMY OF THE WORD

My turn. The history of one of my follies.

For a long time I prided myself on possessing all possible landscapes, and found the celebrities of modern painting and poetry ridiculous.

I loved absurd paintings, panel-friezes, stage settings, clowns' backdrops, signboards, popular colored prints; old-fashioned literature, church Latin, erotic books without proper spelling, novels of our grandmothers' time, fairy tales, little books for children, old operas, silly refrains, artless rhythms.

I dreamt of crusades, voyages of discoveries of which there are no reports, republics without recorded histories, suppressed religious wars, revolutions in morals, movements of races and of continents: I believed in all enchantments.

I invented the color of the vowels! — A black, E white, I red, O blue, U green. — I established rules for the form and movement of each consonant, and, with instinctive rhythms, I flattered myself on devising a poetic language accessible, one day or another, to all the senses. I withheld the translation.

This was at first a study. I wrote down silences, nights, I recorded the inexpressible. I determined vertigoes.

> Remote from birds, from flocks, from country girls,
> What did I drink, while kneeling in that heath
> Surrounded by new growth of hazel trees,
> Within a mild green mist of afternoon?

Que pouvais-je boire dans cette jeune Oise,
— Ormeaux sans voix, gazon sans fleurs, ciel couvert! —
Boire à ces gourdes jaunes, loin de ma case
Chérie? Quelque liqueur d'or qui fait suer.

Je faisais une louche enseigne d'auberge.
— Un orage vint chasser le ciel. Au soir
L'eau des bois se perdait sur les sables vierges,
Le vent de Dieu jetait des glaçons aux mares;

Pleurant, je voyais de l'or — et ne pus boire.

A quatre heures du matin, l'été,
Le sommeil d'amour dure encore.
Sous les bocages s'évapore
    L'odeur du soir fêté.

Là-bas, dans leur vaste chantier
Au soleil des Hespérides,
Déjà s'agitent — en bras de chemise —
    Les Charpentiers.

Dans leurs Déserts de mousse, tranquilles,
Ils préparent les lambris précieux
    Où la ville
    Peindra de faux cieux.

O, pour ces Ouvriers, charmants
Sujets d'un roi de Babylone,
Vénus! quitte un instant les Amants
    Dont l'âme est en couronne.

What could I drink in that young river Oise,
— The voiceless elms, the flowerless turf, dark sky! —
From yellow gourds, far from my cherished hut?
Some golden liquor that induces sweat.

I made a doubtful signboard for an inn.
— A storm arose and stalked the sky. At night
The forest water drained itself in virgin
Sands, God's wind cast drift ice on the ponds;

Weeping, I saw gold — and could not drink.

At four in the morning, in summertime,
The sleep of love still lasts.
From under the groves there emanates
    The scent of the festive night.

Below, in their vast timber-yard
In Hesperidian sun,
Already they bestir themselves —
    The shirt-sleeved Carpenters.

Within their mossy Wilderness, serene,
They set up costly canopies
        On which the town
        Will paint pretended skies.

O, for these Workers, charming
Subjects of a king of Babylon,
Venus! but a moment leave the Lovers
        Whose souls are crowned.

O Reine des Bergers,
Porte aux travailleurs l'eau-de-vie,
Que leurs forces soient en paix
En attendant le bain dans la mer à midi.

La vieillerie poétique avait une bonne part dans mon al-
chimie du verbe.

Je m'habituai à l'hallucination simple: je voyais très franche-
ment une mosquée à la place d'une usine, une école de tam-
bours faite par des anges, des calèches sur les routes du ciel,
un salon au fond d'un lac; les monstres, les mystères; un titre
de vaudeville dressait des épouvantes devant moi.

Puis j'expliquai mes sophismes magiques avec l'hallucination
des mots!

Je finis par trouver sacré le désordre de mon esprit. J'étais
oisif, en proie à une lourde fièvre: j'enviais la félicité des
bêtes, — les chenilles, qui représentent l'innocence des limbes,
les taupes, le sommeil de la virginité!

Mon caractère s'aigrissait. Je disais adieu au monde dans
d'espèces de romances:

CHANSON DE LA PLUS HAUTE TOUR
Qu'il vienne, qu'il vienne,
Le temps dont on s'éprenne.

J'ai tant fait patience
Qu'à jamais j'oublie.
Craintes et souffrances
Aux cieux sont parties.
Et la soif malsaine
Obscurcit mes veines.

O Queen of Shepherds,
Bear brandy to the laborers,
So that their strength may be at peace
Until the dip at midday in the sea.

Old tricks of poetry played a large part in my alchemy of
the word.

I became habituated to pure hallucination: I saw very plainly
a mosque in place of a factory, a school of drummers composed
of angels, open carriages· on the roads of heaven, a drawing
room at the bottom of a lake; monsters, mysteries; a title from
light comedy would raise terrors before me.

Then I explained my magical sophistry with the hallucination of words!

I ended up considering my mental disorder sacred. I was
idle, the prey of a severe fever: I envied the bliss of dumb
creatures, — caterpillars, that represent the innocence of limbo,
and moles, the sleep of virginity!

My nature became embittered. I said farewell to the world
in some kinds of songs:

SONG OF THE HIGHEST TOWER
May it come, may it come,
The time of which we'd be enamored.

I have endured so patiently
That I have lost all memory.
My many fears and sufferings
Have taken flight into the skies.
And now the health-destroying thirst
Is darkening my blood and veins.

Qu'il vienne, qu'il vienne,
Le temps dont on s'éprenne.

Telle la prairie
A l'oubli livrée,
Grandie, et fleurie
D'encens et d'ivraies,
Au bourdon farouche
Des sales mouches.

Qu'il vienne, qu'il vienne,
Le temps dont on s'éprenne.

J'aimai le désert, les vergers brûlés, les boutiques fanées, les boissons tiédies. Je me traînais dans les ruelles puantes et, les yeux fermés, je m'offrais au soleil, dieu de feu.

« Général, s'il reste un vieux canon sur tes remparts en ruine, bombarde-nous avec des blocs de terre sèche. Aux glaces des magasins splendides! dans les salons! Fais manger sa poussière à la ville. Oxyde les gargouilles. Emplis les boudoirs de poudre de rubis brûlante . . . »

Oh! le moucheron enivré à la pissotière de l'auberge, amoureux de la bourrache, et que dissout un rayon!

FAIM

Si j'ai du goût, ce n'est guère
Que pour la terre et les pierres.
Je déjeune toujours d'air,
De roc, de charbons, de fer.

May it come, may it come,
The time of which we'd be enamored.

Such is the meadowland
Delivered to oblivion,
All overgrown, and flowering
With frankincense and tares,
Amid the frantic buzzing
Of the filthy flies.

May it come, may it come,
The time of which we'd be enamored.

I loved the wilderness, parched orchards, faded shops, tepid drinks. I would drag myself through stinking alleys, and, with eyes shut, I would offer myself to the sun, god of fire.

"General, if there remains one old cannon on your ruined ramparts, bombard us with lumps of dried earth. On the windows of splendid shops! into the drawing rooms! Make the town eat its own dust. Oxidize the gargoyles. Fill the boudoirs with the burning powder of rubies. . ."

Oh! the drunken gnat in the urinal of the tavern, infatuated with borage, and dissolved by a sunbeam!

HUNGER

If I have any taste, it is
For earth and stones — not much besides.
Invariably I breakfast so:
On air, on rock, on coal, on iron.

Mes faims, tournez. Paissez, faims,
  Le pré des sons.
  Attirez le gai venin
  Des liserons.

Mangez les cailloux qu'on brise,
Les vieilles pierres d'églises;
Les galets des vieux déluges,
Pains semés dans les vallées grises.

Le loup criait sous les feuilles
En crachant les belles plumes
De son repas de volailles:
Comme lui je me consume.

Les salades, les fruits
N'attendent que la cueillette;
Mais l'araignée de la haie
Ne mange que des violettes.

Que je dorme! que je bouille
Aux autels de Salomon.
Le bouillon court sur la rouille,
Et se mêle au Cédron.

Enfin, ô bonheur, ô raison, j'écartais du ciel l'azur qui est
du noir, et je vécus, étincelle d'or de la lumière *nature*. De
joie, je prenais une expression bouffonne et égarée au possible:

My hungers, turn. Graze, hungers, on
    The meadow of sounds.
Extract the spicy venom from
    The morning-glory cups.

Devour the flintstones crushed to bits,
The ancient stones of churches;
The cobbles left by old-time floods,
Loaves scattered in gray valleys.

The wolf was howling underneath
The leaves, while spitting out fine tufts
Of feathers from his feast of fowl:
And I, like him, consume myself.

The salad greens, the harvest fruits
Are waiting only to be picked;
Whereas the spider of the hedge
Eats nothing but the violets.

Let me sleep! let me seethe
On the altars of Solomon.
The broth runs down upon the rust,
And mingles with the Kedron.

  At last, O happiness, O reason, I removed from the sky the
azure, which is darkness, and I lived, a spark of gold of *pure*
light. Out of joy, I assumed an expression as clownish and
wild as possible:

Elle est retrouvée!
Quoi? l'éternité.
C'est la mer mêlée
  Au soleil.

Mon âme éternelle,
Observe ton vœu
Malgré la nuit seule
Et le jour en feu.

Donc tu te dégages
Des humains suffrages,
Des communs élans!
Tu voles selon . . .

— Jamais l'espérance,
Pas d'*orietur*.
Science et patience,
Le supplice est sûr.

Plus de lendemain,
Braises de satin,
Votre ardeur
Est le devoir.

Elle est retrouvée!
— Quoi? — l'Éternité.
C'est la mer mêlée
  Au soleil.

Je devins un opéra fabuleux: je vis que tous les êtres ont une fatalité de bonheur: l'action n'est pas la vie, mais une façon de gâcher quelque force, un énervement. La morale est la faiblesse de la cervelle.

It is now found once more!
What? eternity.
It is the sea commingled
    With the sun.

My own immortal soul,
Fulfill your vow
Despite the lonely night
And the day on fire.

Thus you detach yourself
From human approbation,
From universal drives!
You soar according to . . .

— No hope evermore,
Nor any *orietur*.
Knowledge and endurance,
Punishment is sure.

No more tomorrow,
Embers of satin,
Your ardor is
The duty you owe.

It is now found once more!
— What? — Eternity.
It is the sea commingled
    With the sun.

I became a fabulous opera: I saw that all beings have a
destined end to happiness: action is not life, but a way of
wasting some force, an enervation. Morality is the weakness
of the brain.

A chaque être, plusieurs *autres* vies me semblaient dues. Ce monsieur ne sait ce qu'il fait: il est un ange. Cette famille est une nichée de chiens. Devant plusieurs hommes, je causai tout haut avec un moment d'une de leurs autres vies. — Ainsi, j'ai aimé un porc.

Aucun des sophismes de la folie, — la folie qu'on enferme, — n'a été oublié par moi: je pourrais les redire tous, je tiens le système.

Ma santé fut menacée. La terreur venait. Je tombais dans des sommeils de plusieurs jours, et, levé, je continuais les rêves les plus tristes. J'étais mûr pour le trépas, et par une route de dangers ma faiblesse me menait aux confins du monde et de la Cimmérie, patrie de l'ombre et des tourbillons.

Je dus voyager, distraire les enchantements assemblés sur mon cerveau. Sur la mer, que j'aimais comme si elle eût dû me laver d'une souillure, je voyais se lever la croix consolatrice. J'avais été damné par l'arc-en-ciel. Le Bonheur était ma fatalité, mon remords, mon ver: ma vie serait toujours trop immense pour être dévouée à la force et à la beauté.

Le Bonheur! Sa dent, douce à la mort, m'avertissait au chant du coq, — *ad matutinum*, au *Christus venit*, — dans les plus sombres villes:

O saisons, ô châteaux!
Quelle âme est sans défauts?

J'ai fait la magique étude
Du bonheur, qu'aucun n'élude.

Salut à lui, chaque fois
Que chante le coq gaulois.

Ah! je n'aurai plus d'envie:
Il s'est chargé de ma vie.

To every being, several *other* lives seemed to me to be due. This gentleman does not know what he is doing: he is an angel. This family is a pack of dogs. In the presence of several men, I conversed quite loudly with a moment from one of their other lives. — Thus, I have loved a pig.

Not one of the sophisms of madness, — the madness that society locks up, — was forgotten by me: I could repeat them all, I understand the system.

My health was threatened. Terror developed. I fell into sleeps of several days' duration, and, when up, I continued the saddest dreams. I was ripe for death, and by a road of dangers my weakness led me to the ends of the world and of Cimmeria, the home of darkness and of whirlwinds.

I had to travel, to divert the enchantments collected in my brain. Upon the sea, which I loved as if it could have cleansed me of a defilement, I saw the consoling cross arise. I had been damned by the rainbow. Happiness was my fatality, my remorse, my worm: my life would always be too vast to be devoted to strength and to beauty.

Happiness! Its tooth, sweet unto death, warned me at cock-crow, — *ad matutinum*, at the *Christus venit*, — in the darkest cities:

> O seasons, O châteaux!
> What soul is quite unflawed?
>
> I have pursued the magic lore
> Of happiness, which all explore.
>
> Hail to it, every time
> The Gallic cock announces dawn.
>
> Ah! I shall have no more desire:
> It has taken charge of my life entire.

Ce charme a pris âme et corps
Et dispersé les efforts.

O saisons, ô châteaux!

L'heure de sa fuite, hélas!
Sera l'heure du trépas.

O saisons, ô châteaux!

Cela s'est passé. Je sais aujourd'hui saluer la beauté.

That charm has captured soul and body
And dissipated my endeavors.

O seasons, O châteaux!

Alas! the hour that it flies
Will be the hour of my demise.

O seasons, O châteaux!

That is finished. I know today how to hail beauty.

L'Impossible

Ah! cette vie de mon enfance, la grande route par tous les temps, sobre surnaturellement, plus désintéressé que le meilleur des mendiants, fier de n'avoir ni pays, ni amis, quelle sottise c'était. — Et je m'en aperçois seulement!

— J'ai eu raison de mépriser ces bonshommes qui ne perdraient pas l'occasion d'une caresse, parasites de la propreté et de la santé de nos femmes, aujourd'hui qu'elles sont si peu d'accord avec nous.

J'ai eu raison dans tous mes dédains: puisque je m'évade!

Je m'évade!

Je m'explique.

Hier encore, je soupirais: « Ciel! sommes-nous assez de damnés ici-bas! Moi, j'ai tant de temps déjà dans leur troupe! Je les connais tous. Nous nous reconnaissons toujours; nous nous dégoûtons. La charité nous est inconnue. Mais nous sommes polis; nos relations avec le monde sont très-convenables. » Est-ce étonnant? Le monde! les marchands, les naïfs! — Nous ne sommes pas déshonorés. — Mais les élus, comment nous recevraient-ils? Or il y a des gens hargneux et joyeux, de faux élus, puisqu'il nous faut de l'audace ou de l'humilité pour les aborder. Ce sont les seuls élus. Ce ne sont pas des bénisseurs!

M'étant retrouvé deux sous de raison — ça passe vite! — je vois que mes malaises viennent de ne m'être pas figuré assez tôt que nous sommes à l'Occident. Les marais occidentaux! Non que je croie la lumière altérée, la forme exténuée, le mouvement égaré . . . Bon! voici que mon esprit veut absolument se charger de tous les développements cruels qu'a subis l'esprit depuis la fin de l'Orient . . . Il en veut, mon esprit!

The Impossible

Ah! that life of my childhood, the highway in all weathers, supernaturally sober, more disinterested than the best of beggars, proud to have neither country nor friends, what stupidity it was. — And I perceive it only now!

— I was right to scorn those simple-minded men who never would lose the opportunity for a caress, parasites on the cleanliness and health of our women, today when they are so little in harmony with us.

I was right in all my disdain: since I am escaping!

I am escaping!

This is what I mean.

Only yesterday, I was sighing: "Heavens! there are enough of us damned souls down here! As for me, I have already spent so much time with that crowd! I know them all. We always recognize one another; we disgust one another. Charity is unknown to us. But we are polite; our relations with people are most proper." Is that surprising? People! merchants, simpletons! — We are not dishonored. — But the elect, how would they receive us? Now there are fretful and joyful people, a false elect, since we need audacity or humility to approach them. These are the only elect. They are not those who bless!

Having recovered two cents' worth of reason — it disappears quickly! — I see that my discomforts come from not having realized soon enough that we are in the West. The western marshes! Not that I believe the light dimmed, the form weakened, the movement misled . . . Fine! see how my spirit insists on charging itself with all the cruel developments which the spirit has undergone since the end of the East. . . It insists, my spirit!

. . . Mes deux sous de raison sont finis! — L'esprit est autorité, il veut que je sois en Occident. Il faudrait le faire taire pour conclure comme je voulais.

J'envoyais au diable les palmes des martyrs, les rayons de l'art, l'orgueil des inventeurs, l'ardeur des pillards; je retournais à l'Orient et à la sagesse première et éternelle. — Il paraît que c'est un rêve de paresse grossière!

Pourtant, je ne songeais guère au plaisir d'échapper aux souffrances modernes. Je n'avais pas en vue la sagesse bâtarde du Coran. — Mais n'y a-t-il pas un supplice réel en ce que, depuis cette déclaration de la science, le christianisme, l'homme *se joue*, se prouve les évidences, se gonfle du plaisir de répéter ces preuves, et ne vit que comme cela! Torture subtile, niaise; source de mes divagations spirituelles. La nature pourrait s'ennuyer, peut-être! M. Prudhomme est né avec le Christ.

N'est-ce pas parce que nous cultivons la brume! Nous mangeons la fièvre avec nos légumes aqueux. Et l'ivrognerie! et le tabac! et l'ignorance! et les dévouements! — Tout cela est-il assez loin de la pensée, de la sagesse de l'Orient, la patrie primitive? Pourquoi un monde moderne, si de pareils poisons s'inventent!

Les gens d'Église diront: C'est compris. Mais vous voulez parler de l'Éden. Rien pour vous dans l'histoire des peuples orientaux. — C'est vrai; c'est à l'Éden que je songeais! Qu'est-ce que c'est pour mon rêve, cette pureté des races antiques!

Les philosophes: Le monde n'a pas d'âge. L'humanité se déplace, simplement. Vous êtes en Occident, mais libre d'habiter dans votre Orient, quelque ancien qu'il vous le faille, — et d'y habiter bien. Ne soyez pas un vaincu. Philosophes, vous êtes de votre Occident.

Mon esprit, prends garde. Pas de partis de salut violents. Exerce-toi! — Ah! la science ne va pas assez vite pour nous!

. . . My two cents' worth of reason is spent! — The spirit is the authority, it insists that I be in the West. I'd have to silence it to decide as I wished.

I sent to the devil the palms of martyrs, the splendors of art, the pride of inventors, the ardor of pillagers; I returned to the East and to the first and eternal wisdom. — It appears to be a dream of gross indolence!

Nevertheless, I hardly thought about the delight of escaping from modern sufferings. I did not have in mind the bastard wisdom of the Koran. — But is there not real torment in the fact that, since that declaration of knowledge, Christianity, man *deceives himself*, proves obvious ideas to himself, puffs himself up with the pleasure of repeating these proofs, and lives only like that! Subtle, foolish torture; source of my spiritual wanderings. Nature might get bored, perhaps! M. Prudhomme was born with Christ.

Isn't it because we cultivate the fog! We consume fever with our watery vegetables. And drunkenness! and tobacco! and ignorance! and devotions! — Is all that far enough away from the thought, from the wisdom of the East, the primeval birthplace? Why a modern world, if such poisons are invented!

Churchmen will say: It is understood. But you wish to speak of Eden. Nothing for you in the history of the Oriental peoples. — It's true; it's of Eden that I was thinking! What does it have to do with my dream, that purity of the ancient races!

Philosophers: The world has no age. Humanity simply moves about. You are in the West, but free to reside in your East, as ancient as you require, — and to live well there. Do not be a loser. Philosophers, you belong to your West.

My spirit, take care. No violent resolutions on salvation. Exert yourself! — Ah! science does not go fast enough for us!

— Mais je m'aperçois que mon esprit dort.

S'il était bien éveillé toujours à partir de ce moment, nous serions bientôt à la vérité, qui peut-être nous entoure avec ses anges pleurant! . . . — S'il avait été éveillé jusqu'à ce moment-ci, c'est que je n'aurais pas cédé aux instincts délétères, à une époque immémoriale! . . . — S'il avait toujours été bien éveillé, je voguerais en pleine sagesse! . . .

O pureté! pureté!

C'est cette minute d'éveil qui m'a donné la vision de la pureté! — Par l'esprit on va à Dieu!

Déchirante infortune!

— But I notice that my spirit is asleep.

If it were always wide awake from this moment on, we'd soon come to the truth, which perhaps surrounds us with its angels weeping! . . . — If it had been awake until this very moment, it's true that I would not have yielded to deleterious instincts, in an immemorial age! . . . — If it had always been wide awake, I'd be sailing in complete wisdom! . . .

O purity! purity!

It is this moment of awakening which has given me the vision of purity! — Through the spirit one reaches God!

Harrowing misfortune!

L'Éclair

Le travail humain! c'est l'explosion qui éclaire mon abîme de temps en temps.

« Rien n'est vanité; à la science, et en avant! » crie l'Ecclésiaste moderne, c'est-à-dire *Tout le monde.* Et pourtant les cadavres des méchants et des fainéants tombent sur le cœur des autres . . . Ah! vite, vite un peu; là-bas, par delà la nuit, ces récompenses futures, éternelles . . . les échappons-nous? . . .

— Qu'y puis-je? Je connais le travail; et la science est trop lente. Que la prière galope et que la lumière gronde . . . je le vois bien. C'est trop simple, et il fait trop chaud; on se passera de moi. J'ai mon devoir, j'en serai fier à la façon de plusieurs, en le mettant de côté.

Ma vie est usée. Allons! feignons, fainéantons, ô pitié! Et nous existerons en nous amusant, en rêvant amours monstres et univers fantastiques, en nous plaignant et en querellant les apparences du monde, saltimbanque, mendiant, artiste, bandit, — prêtre! Sur mon lit d'hôpital, l'odeur de l'encens m'est revenue si puissante; gardien des aromates sacrés, confesseur, martyr . . .

Je reconnais là ma sale éducation d'enfance. Puis quoi! . . . Aller mes vingt ans, si les autres vont vingt ans . . .

Non! non! à présent je me révolte contre la mort! Le travail paraît trop léger à mon orgueil: ma trahison au monde serait un supplice trop court. Au dernier moment, j'attaquerais à droite, à gauche . . .

Alors, — oh! chère pauvre âme, l'éternité serait-elle pas perdue pour nous!

The Flash of Lightning

Human toil! this is the explosion that illuminates my abyss from time to time.

"Nothing is vanity; on to science, and forward!" cries the modern Ecclesiast, that is to say *Everyone*. And yet the corpses of the evil and of the slothful fall upon the hearts of others . . . Ah! quickly, rather quickly; over there, beyond the night, those future rewards, everlasting . . . shall we shun them? . . .

— What can I do? I know work; and science is too slow. Let prayer gallop and let light roar . . . I see it plainly. It is too simple, and the weather is too warm; they will do without me. I have my duty, I shall be proud of it after the fashion of some people, by setting it aside.

My life is worn out. Come! let us dissemble, let us loaf, O mercy! And we shall exist by amusing ourselves, by dreaming of monstrous loves and fantastic universes, by complaining and quarreling with the pretenses of the world: buffoon, beggar, artist, bandit, — priest! On my hospital bed, the odor of incense, so overpowering, came back to me; guardian of the holy aromatics, confessor, martyr . . .

I recognize there my foul upbringing. What of it! . . . To reach my twenty years, if others are reaching twenty years . . .

No! no! right now I rebel against death! Work seems too trivial to my pride: my betrayal to the world would be too brief a torture. At the last moment, I'd attack on the right, on the left . . .

Then, — oh! poor dear soul, would eternity not be lost to us!

99

Matin

N'eus-je pas *une fois* une jeunesse aimable, héroïque, fabuleuse, à écrire sur des feuilles d'or, — trop de chance! Par quel crime, par quelle erreur, ai-je mérité ma faiblesse actuelle? Vous qui prétendez que des bêtes poussent des sanglots de chagrin, que des malades désespèrent, que des morts rêvent mal, tâchez de raconter ma chute et mon sommeil. Moi, je ne puis pas plus m'expliquer que le mendiant avec ses continuels *Pater* et *Ave Maria. Je ne sais plus parler!*

Pourtant, aujourd'hui, je crois avoir fini la relation de mon enfer. C'était bien l'enfer; l'ancien, celui dont le fils de l'homme ouvrit les portes.

Du même désert, à la même nuit, toujours mes yeux las se réveillent à l'étoile d'argent, toujours, sans que s'émeuvent les Rois de la vie, les trois mages, le cœur, l'âme, l'esprit. Quand irons-nous, par delà les grèves et les monts, saluer la naissance du travail nouveau, la sagesse nouvelle, la fuite des tyrans et des démons, la fin de la superstition, adorer — les premiers! — Noël sur la terre!

Le chant des cieux, la marche des peuples! Esclaves, ne maudissons pas la vie.

Morning

Did I not *once* have a lovely youth, heroic, fabulous, to be inscribed on leaves of gold, — too much luck! Through what crime, through what error, have I deserved my present weakness? You who maintain that animals heave sobs of grief, that the sick despair, that the dead have bad dreams, try to recount my fall and my sleep. As for me, I can no more explain myself than the beggar with his perpetual *Paters* and *Ave Marias*. *I no longer know how to speak!*

Today, however, I think I have finished the account of my hell. It surely was hell; the old one, the one whose gates the son of man opened.

From the same wilderness, in the same night, always my tired eyes waken to the silver star, always, although the Kings of life, the three magi, the heart, the soul, the mind, are not moved. When shall we go, beyond the shores and the mountains, to acclaim the birth of the new work, the new wisdom, the flight of tyrants and of demons, the end of superstition, to adore — the first worshipers! — Christmas on earth!

The song of the heavens, the procession of peoples! Slaves, let us not blaspheme life.

Adieu

L'automne déjà! — Mais pourquoi regretter un éternel soleil, si nous sommes engagés à la découverte de la clarté divine, — loin des gens qui meurent sur les saisons.

L'automne. Notre barque élevée dans les brumes immobiles tourne vers le port de la misère, la cité énorme au ciel taché de feu et de boue. Ah! les haillons pourris, le pain trempé de pluie, l'ivresse, les mille amours qui m'ont crucifié! Elle ne finira donc point cette goule reine de millions d'âmes et de corps morts *et qui seront jugés!* Je me revois la peau rongée par la boue et la peste, des vers plein les cheveux et les aisselles et encore de plus gros vers dans le cœur, étendu parmi les inconnus sans âge, sans sentiment . . . J'aurais pu y mourir . . . L'affreuse évocation! J'exècre la misère.

Et je redoute l'hiver parce que c'est la saison du confort!

— Quelquefois je vois au ciel des plages sans fin couvertes de blanches nations en joie. Un grand vaisseau d'or, au-dessus de moi, agite ses pavillons multicolores sous les brises du matin. J'ai créé toutes les fêtes, tous les triomphes, tous les drames. J'ai essayé d'inventer de nouvelles fleurs, de nouveaux astres, de nouvelles chairs, de nouvelles langues. J'ai cru acquérir des pouvoirs surnaturels. Eh bien! je dois enterrer mon imagination et mes souvenirs! Une belle gloire d'artiste et de conteur emportée!

Moi! moi qui me suis dit mage ou ange, dispensé de toute morale, je suis rendu au sol, avec un devoir à chercher, et la réalité rugueuse à étreindre! Paysan!

Suis-je trompé? la charité serait-elle sœur de la mort, pour moi?

Farewell

Autumn already! — But why yearn for an eternal sun, if we are committed to the discovery of divine light, — far from the people who die by the seasons.

Autumn. Our boat lifted up through the motionless mists turns toward the port of poverty, the enormous city with its sky stained by fire and mud. Ah! the putrid rags, the rain-drenched bread, the drunkenness, the thousand loves that have crucified me! Will she not stop at all, then, this ghoul queen of millions of souls and of dead bodies *which will be judged!* I see myself again, my skin pitted by mud and pestilence, my hair and my armpits full of worms, and even bigger worms in my heart, lying among strangers without age, without feeling . . . I could have died there . . . Frightful recollection! I abhor poverty.

And I dread winter because it is the season of comfort!

— Sometimes I see in the sky endless beaches covered with joyful white nations. A great golden ship, above me, waves its multicolored pennants in the morning breezes. I have created all festivals, all triumphs, all dramas. I have tried to invent new flowers, new stars, new flesh, new tongues. I believed I acquired supernatural powers. Well! I must bury my imagination and my memories! A great glory as an artist and storyteller swept away!

I! I who called myself a seer or an angel, exempt from all morality, I am restored to the earth, with a duty to seek, and rugged reality to embrace! Peasant!

Am I deceived? would charity be the sister of death, for me?

Enfin, je demanderai pardon pour m'être nourri de mensonge. Et allons.

Mais pas une main amie! et où puiser le secours?

Oui, l'heure nouvelle est au moins très-sévère.

Car je puis dire que la victoire m'est acquise: les grincements de dents, les sifflements de feu, les soupirs empestés se modèrent. Tous les souvenirs immondes s'effacent. Mes derniers regrets détalent, — des jalousies pour les mendiants, les brigands, les amis de la mort, les arriérés de toutes sortes. — Damnés, si je me vengeais!

Il faut être absolument moderne.

Point de cantiques: tenir le pas gagné. Dure nuit! le sang séché fume sur ma face, et je n'ai rien derrière moi, que cet horrible arbrisseau! . . . Le combat spirituel est aussi brutal que la bataille d'hommes; mais la vision de la justice est le plaisir de Dieu seul.

Cependant c'est la veille. Recevons tous les influx de vigueur et de tendresse réelle. Et à l'aurore, armés d'une ardente patience, nous entrerons aux splendides villes.

Que parlais-je de main amie! Un bel avantage, c'est que je puis rire des vieilles amours mensongères, et frapper de honte ces couples menteurs, — j'ai vu l'enfer des femmes là-bas; — et il me sera loisible de *posséder la vérité dans une âme et un corps.*

Avril-août 1873

Finally, I shall beg pardon for having nourished myself on falsehood. Then let's go.

But not one friendly hand! and where am I to draw help?

Yes, the new hour is at the least very harsh.

For I can say that victory is won for me: the gnashings of teeth, the hissings of fire, the reeking sighs are subsiding. All the foul memories are fading away. My last regrets are scampering off, — jealousies for beggars, brigands, friends of death, backward characters of all sorts. — Damned creatures, if I avenged myself!

One must be absolutely modern.

No hymns: keep the stride made. Hard night! dried blood smokes on my face, and I have nothing behind me, but that horrible bush! . . . Spiritual combat is as brutal as the battle of men; but the vision of justice is the delight of God alone.

Meanwhile this is the eve. Let us receive all influxes of vigor and of real tenderness. And at dawn, armed with an ardent patience, we shall enter the splendid cities.

What was I saying about a friendly hand! One great advantage is that I can laugh at the old false loves, and smite with shame those deceitful couples, — I have seen the hell of women down there; — and it will be permissible for me *to possess truth in one soul and one body*.

April–August 1873

Les Illuminations

The Illuminations

I
Après le déluge

Aussitôt que l'idée du Déluge se fut rassise, un lièvre s'arrêta dans les sainfoins et les clochettes mouvantes, et dit sa prière à l'arc-en-ciel à travers la toile de l'araignée.

Oh! les pierres précieuses qui se cachaient, — les fleurs qui regardaient déjà.

Dans la grande rue sale les étals se dressèrent, et l'on tira les barques vers la mer étagée là-haut comme sur les gravures.

Le sang coula, chez Barbe-Bleue, — aux abattoirs, — dans les cirques, où le sceau de Dieu blêmit les fenêtres. Le sang et le lait coulèrent.

Les castors bâtirent. Les « mazagrans » fumèrent dans les estaminets.

Dans la grande maison de vitres encore ruisselante, les enfants en deuil regardèrent les merveilleuses images.

Une porte claqua, et, sur la place du hameau, l'enfant tourna ses bras, compris des girouettes et des coqs des clochers de partout, sous l'éclatante giboulée.

Madame*** établit un piano dans les Alpes. La messe et les premières communions se célébrèrent aux cent mille autels de la cathédrale.

Les caravanes partirent. Et le Splendide-Hôtel fut bâti dans le chaos de glaces et de nuit du pôle.

Depuis lors, la Lune entendit les chacals piaulant par les déserts de thym — et les églogues en sabots grognant dans le verger. Puis, dans la futaie violette, bourgeonnante, Eucharis me dit que c'était le printemps.

I
After the Flood

As soon as the idea of the Flood had subsided, a hare paused among the sainfoins and the swaying bellflowers, and said his prayer to the rainbow through the spider's web.

Oh! the precious stones that were hiding, — the flowers that already looked around.

In the filthy main street butchers' stalls rose, and barges were tugged toward the sea rising up in tiers as in engravings.

Blood flowed, at Bluebeard's,— in slaughterhouses, — in circuses, where the seal of God whitened the windows. Blood and milk flowed.

Beavers did their building. Glasses of black coffee steamed in the cafés.

In the still dripping big house with glass panes, children in mourning looked at the marvelous reflections.

A door slammed, and, in the village square, the child waved his arms, understood by weather vanes and cocks on steeples everywhere, under the glittering downpour.

Madame * * * installed a piano in the Alps. Mass and first communions were celebrated at the hundred thousand altars of the cathedral.

Caravans departed. And the Hotel Splendide was erected in the chaos of ice and of polar night.

From that time, the Moon heard jackals howling through the wildernesses of thyme — and eclogues in wooden shoes grumbling in the orchard. Then, in the forest, violet-hued, burgeoning, Eucharis told me that it was spring.

Sourds, étang; — Écume, roule sur le pont et par-dessus les bois; — draps noirs et orgues, — éclairs et tonnerre, — montez et roulez; — Eaux et tristesses, montez et relevez les Déluges.

Car depuis qu'ils se sont dissipés, — oh! les pierres précieuses s'enfouissant, et les fleurs ouvertes! — c'est un ennui! et la Reine, la Sorcière qui allume sa braise dans le pot de terre, ne voudra jamais nous raconter ce qu'elle sait, et que nous ignorons.

II
Enfance

I

Cette idole, yeux noirs et crin jaune, sans parents ni cour, plus noble que la fable, mexicaine et flamande: son domaine, azur et verdure insolents, court sur des plages nommées par des vagues sans vaisseaux de noms férocement grecs, slaves, celtiques.

A la lisière de la forêt — les fleurs de rêve tintent, éclatent, éclairent, — la fille à lèvre d'orange, les genoux croisés dans le clair déluge qui sourd des prés, nudité qu'ombrent, traversent et habillent les arcs-en-ciel, la flore, la mer.

Dames qui tournoient sur les terrasses voisines de la mer; enfantes et géantes, superbes noires dans la mousse vert-de-gris, bijoux debout sur le sol gras des bosquets et des jardinets dégelés, — jeunes mères et grandes sœurs aux regards pleins de pèlerinages, sultanes, princesses de démarche et de costumes tyranniques, petites étrangères et personnes doucement malheureuses.

Quel ennui, l'heure du « cher corps » et « cher cœur »!

Gush forth, pond; — Foam, roll above the bridge and over the woods; — black palls and organs, — lightning and thunder, — rise up and roll; — Waters and sorrows, rise up and release the Floods again.

For since they have vanished, — oh! the precious stones burying themselves, and the opened flowers! — it's a nuisance! and the Queen, the Sorceress who kindles her coals in the earthen pot, will never be willing to tell us what she knows, and what we do not know.

II
Childhood

I

That idol, black eyes and yellow mane, without kinsmen or court, more noble than fable, Mexican and Flemish: his domain, insolent azure and verdure, extends over the beaches named by the waves without ships with names fiercely Greek, Slav, Celtic.

At the edge of the forest — the dream flowers tinkle, sparkle, illuminate, — the girl with orange lip, her knees crossed in the clear flood that gushes from the meadows, nakedness which the rainbows, the flora, the sea shade, traverse and clothe.

Ladies who turn round and round on the terraces adjacent to the sea; little girls and giantesses, superb black women in the verdigris moss, jewels upright on the rich earth of the groves and of the thawed small gardens, — young mothers and grown-up sisters with glances full of pilgrimages, sultanas, princesses tyrannical in bearing and in dress, little foreign girls and persons quietly unhappy.

What a bore, the hour of the "dear body" and "dear heart"!

II

C'est elle, la petite morte, derrière les rosiers. — La jeune maman trépassée descend le perron. — La calèche du cousin crie sur le sable. — Le petit frère — (il est aux Indes!) là, devant le couchant, sur le pré d'œillets. — Les vieux qu'on a enterrés tout droits dans le rempart aux giroflées.

L'essaim des feuilles d'or entoure la maison du général. Ils sont dans le midi. — On suit la route rouge pour arriver à l'auberge vide. Le château est à vendre; les persiennes sont détachées. — Le curé aura emporté la clef de l'église. — Autour du parc, les loges des gardes sont inhabitées. Les palissades sont si hautes qu'on ne voit que les cimes bruissantes. D'ailleurs, il n'y a rien à voir là-dedans.

Les prés remontent aux hameaux sans coqs, sans enclumes. L'écluse est levée. O les calvaires et les moulins du désert, les îles et les meules.

Des fleurs magiques bourdonnaient. Les talus le berçaient. Des bêtes d'une élégance fabuleuse circulaient. Les nuées s'amassaient sur la haute mer faite d'une éternité de chaudes larmes.

III

Au bois, il y a un oiseau, son chant vous arrête et vous fait rougir.

Il y a une horloge qui ne sonne pas.

Il y a une fondrière avec un nid de bêtes blanches.

Il y a une cathédrale qui descend et un lac qui monte.

Il y a une petite voiture abandonnée dans le taillis, ou qui descend le sentier en courant, enrubannée.

Il y a une troupe de petits comédiens en costumes, aperçus sur la route à travers la lisière du bois.

Il y a enfin, quand l'on a faim et soif, quelqu'un qui vous chasse.

II

It's she, the little dead girl, behind the rosebushes. — The deceased young mamma descends the flight of steps. — The cousin's carriage creaks on the sand. — The little brother — (he's in the Indies!) there, against the sunset, in the meadow of pinks. — The old men who have been buried upright in the rampart with the gillyflowers.

The swarm of golden leaves encircles the general's house. They are in the south. — One follows the red road to arrive at the empty inn. The castle is for sale; the shutters are unhinged. — The parish priest must have taken away the key of the church. — Around the park, the keepers' lodges are uninhabited. The fences are so high that one sees only the rustling treetops. Besides, there is nothing to see inside.

The meadows rise again to the hamlets without weathercocks, without anvils. The floodgate is raised. O the calvaries and the mills of the wilderness, the islands and the millstones.

Magic flowers were murmuring. Embankments cradled him. Beasts of a fabulous elegance moved around. Storm clouds accumulated over the high sea made of an eternity of bitter tears.

III

In the woods, there is a bird; his song arrests you and makes you blush.

There is a clock that does not strike.

There is a gully with a nest of white beasts.

There is a cathedral that descends and a lake that rises.

There is a little carriage abandoned in the thicket, or which, adorned with ribbons, goes racing down the path.

There is a company of little actors in costumes, glimpsed on the road through the edge of the woods.

There is, finally, when you are hungry and thirsty, someone who chases you away.

IV

Je suis le saint, en prière sur la terrasse, — comme les bêtes pacifiques paissent jusqu'à la mer de Palestine.

Je suis le savant au fauteuil sombre. Les branches et la pluie se jettent à la croisée de la bibliothèque.

Je suis le piéton de la grand'route par les bois nains; la rumeur des écluses couvre mes pas. Je vois longtemps la mélancolique lessive d'or du couchant.

Je serais bien l'enfant abandonné sur la jetée partie à la haute mer, le petit valet suivant l'allée dont le front touche le ciel.

Les sentiers sont âpres. Les monticules se couvrent de genêts. L'air est immobile. Que les oiseaux et les sources sont loin! Ce ne peut être que la fin du monde, en avançant.

V

Qu'on me loue enfin ce tombeau, blanchi à la chaux avec les lignes du ciment en relief, — très loin sous terre.

Je m'accoude à la table, la lampe éclaire très vivement ces journaux que je suis idiot de relire, ces livres sans intérêt.

A une distance énorme au-dessus de mon salon souterrain, les maisons s'implantent, les brumes s'assemblent. La boue est rouge ou noire. Ville monstrueuse, nuit sans fin!

Moins haut, sont des égouts. Aux côtés, rien que l'épaisseur du globe. Peut-être des gouffres d'azur, des puits de feu. C'est peut-être sur ces plans que se rencontrent lunes et comètes, mers et fables.

Aux heures d'amertume je m'imagine des boules de saphir, de métal. Je suis maître du silence. Pourquoi une apparence de soupirail blêmirait-elle au coin de la voûte?

IV

I am the saint, at prayer on the terrace, — as the peaceful beasts graze even to the sea of Palestine.

I am the scholar in the dark armchair. The branches and the rain fling themselves at the casement of the library.

I am the pedestrian on the highway through the stunted woods; the din of the floodgates muffles my steps. I view for a long time the melancholy golden wash of the sunset.

I could well be the child abandoned on the jetty washed away to the high sea, the little valet following the lane whose brow touches the sky.

The paths are rough. The knolls are covered with broom. The air is motionless. How far away are the birds and the springs! It can only be the end of the world, ahead.

V

Let them at last rent me this tomb, whitewashed with lines of cement in relief, — very far under the ground.

I lean on my elbows at the table; the lamp very vividly lights up these newspapers which I'm an idiot to reread, these uninteresting books.

At an enormous distance above my subterranean drawing room, houses take root, fogs gather. The mud is red or black. Monstrous city, night without end!

Not so high up, are the sewers. At the sides, nothing but the thickness of the globe. Perhaps whirlpools of azure, wells of fire. It is perhaps on these planes that moons and comets, seas and fables meet.

In hours of bitterness I imagine balls of sapphire, of metal. I am master of the silence. Why would an appearance of a vent grow pale in the corner of the vault?

III
Conte

Un Prince était vexé de ne s'être employé jamais qu'à la perfection des générosités vulgaires. Il prévoyait d'étonnantes
révolutions de l'amour, et soupçonnait ses femmes de pouvoir
mieux que cette complaisance agrémentée de ciel et de luxe.
Il voulait voir la vérité, l'heure du désir et de la satisfaction
essentiels. Que ce fût ou non une aberration de piété, il voulut.
Il possédait au moins un assez large pouvoir humain.

Toutes les femmes qui l'avaient connu furent assassinées.
Quel saccage du jardin de la beauté! Sous le sabre, elles le
bénirent. Il n'en commanda point de nouvelles. — Les femmes
réapparurent.

Il tua tous ceux qui le suivaient, après la chasse ou les libations. — Tous le suivaient.

Il s'amusa à égorger les bêtes de luxe. Il fit flamber les palais.
Il se ruait sur les gens et les taillait en pièces. — La foule, les
toits d'or, les belles bêtes existaient encore.

Peut-on s'extasier dans la destruction, se rajeunir par la
cruauté! Le peuple ne murmura pas. Personne n'offrit le con-
cours de ses vues.

Un soir il galopait fièrement. Un Génie apparut, d'une
beauté ineffable, inavouable même. De sa physionomie et de
son maintien ressortait la promesse d'un amour multiple et
complexe! d'un bonheur indicible, insupportable même! Le
Prince et le Génie s'anéantirent probablement dans la santé
essentielle. Comment n'auraient-ils pas pu en mourir? Ensemble donc ils moururent.

III
Tale

A Prince was vexed at never having occupied himself with anything but the perfection of ordinary generosities. He foresaw astonishing revolutions in love, and suspected his wives of being capable of something better than that complaisance adorned by heaven and by luxury. He demanded to see the truth, the hour of essential desire and satisfaction. Whether or not this was an aberration of piety, he demanded it. He possessed at least a rather large human power.

All the women who had known him were assassinated. What havoc in the garden of beauty! Under the sword, they blessed him. He did not order any new ones. — The women reappeared.

He killed all those who followed him, after the hunt or the libations. — All followed him.

He amused himself by butchering beasts of luxury. He made palaces burn. He hurled himself at people and hacked them to pieces. — The crowd, the golden roofs, the beautiful beasts still subsisted.

Can one go into ecstasies over destruction, be rejuvenated by cruelty! The people did not murmur. No one offered the assistance of his own views.

One evening he was galloping proudly. A Genie appeared, of a beauty ineffable, undeclarable even. From his physiognomy and from his bearing issued the promise of a love manifold and complex! of a happiness inexpressible, insupportable even! The Prince and the Genie destroyed one another probably in essential health. How could they not have died of it? Together, then, they died.

Mais ce Prince décéda, dans son palais, à un âge ordinaire.
Le Prince était le Génie. Le Génie était le Prince.
La musique savante manque à notre désir.

IV
Parade

Des drôles très solides. Plusieurs ont exploité vos mondes. Sans besoins, et peu pressés de mettre en œuvre leurs brillantes facultés et leur expérience de vos consciences. Quels hommes mûrs! Des yeux hébétés à la façon de la nuit d'été, rouges et noirs, tricolores, d'acier piqué d'étoiles d'or; des faciès déformés, plombés, blêmis, incendiés; des enrouements folâtres! La démarche cruelle des oripeaux! — Il y a quelques jeunes, — comment regarderaient-ils Chérubin? — pourvus de voix effrayantes et de quelques ressources dangereuses. On les envoie prendre du dos en ville, affublés d'un *luxe* dégoûtant.

O le plus violent Paradis de la grimace enragée! Pas de comparaison avec vos Fakirs et les autres bouffonneries scéniques. Dans des costumes improvisés avec le goût du mauvais rêve ils jouent des complaintes, des tragédies de malandrins et de demi-dieux spirituels comme l'histoire ou les religions ne l'ont jamais été. Chinois, Hottentots, bohémiens, niais, hyènes, Molochs, vieilles démences, démons sinistres, ils mêlent les tours populaires, maternels, avec les poses et les tendresses bestiales. Ils interpréteraient des pièces nouvelles et des chansons « bonnes filles ». Maîtres jongleurs, ils transforment le lieu et les personnes et usent de la comédie magnétique. Les yeux flambent, le sang chante, les os s'élargissent, les larmes et des filets rouges ruissellent. Leur raillerie ou leur terreur dure une minute, ou des mois entiers.

J'ai seul la clef de cette parade sauvage.

But this Prince expired, in his palace, at a normal age. The Prince was the Genie. The Genie was the Prince.

Masterly music disappoints our desire.

IV
Pageant

Very robust rascals. Several have exploited your worlds. Without needs, and scarcely pressed to put to work their brilliant faculties and their knowledge of your consciences. What mature men! Their eyes dazed like the summer night, red and black, tricolored, steel pierced with stars of gold; their features deformed, leaden, blanched, burning; sportive hoarsenesses! The cruel gait of flashy finery! — There are some young ones, — how would they regard Chérubin? — possessed of frightful voices and some dangerous expedients. Rigged out in a disgusting *luxury*, they are sent to strut in the town.

O the most violent Paradise of the enraged grimace! No comparison with your Fakirs and the other theatrical buffooneries. In costumes improvised with nightmarish taste they enact mournful ballads, tragedies of brigands and of demigods spiritual as history or religions have never been. Chinese, Hottentots, bohemians, simpletons, hyenas, Molochs, old lunacies, sinister demons, they mix popular, maternal tricks with bestial poses and caresses. They would interpret new plays and "sentimental" songs. Master jugglers, they transform the place and the characters and employ hypnotic theater. Eyes blaze, blood sings, bones broaden, tears and red rivulets stream down. Their raillery or their terror lasts a minute, or entire months.

I alone possess the key of this wild pageant.

V
Antique

Gracieux fils de Pan! Autour de ton front couronné de fleu-
rettes et de baies tes yeux, des boules précieuses, remuent.
Tachées de lies brunes, tes joues se creusent. Tes crocs luisent.
Ta poitrine ressemble à une cithare, des tintements circulent
dans tes bras blonds. Ton cœur bat dans ce ventre où dort le
double sexe. Promène-toi, la nuit, en mouvant doucement
cette cuisse, cette seconde cuisse et cette jambe de gauche.

VI
Being Beauteous

Devant une neige un Être de Beauté de haute taille. Des sifflements de mort et des cercles de musique sourde font monter,
s'élargir et trembler comme un spectre ce corps adoré; des
blessures écarlates et noires éclatent dans les chairs superbes.
Les couleurs propres de la vie se foncent, dansent, et se déga-
gent autour de la Vision, sur le chantier. Et les frissons s'élè-
vent et grondent, et la saveur forcenée de ces effets se chargeant
avec les sifflements mortels et les rauques musiques que le
monde, loin derrière nous, lance sur notre mère de beauté, —
elle recule, elle se dresse. Oh! nos os sont revêtus d'un nouveau
corps amoureux.

*

*　　　*

O la face cendrée, l'écusson de crin, les bras de cristal! le
canon sur lequel je dois m'abattre à travers la mêlée des arbres
et de l'air léger!

V
Antique

Gracious son of Pan! About your brow crowned with flowerets and with berries, your eyes, those precious orbs, move. Stained with brown lees, your cheeks grow gaunt. Your fangs gleam. Your chest resembles a zither, tinklings circulate through your fair arms. Your heart beats in that womb where the double sex sleeps. Walk, at night, gently moving that thigh, that second thigh and that left leg.

VI
Being Beauteous

Against the snow an Incarnation of Beauty of tall stature. Whistlings of death and rounds of muffled' music make this adored body rise, swell and tremble like a ghost; wounds, scarlet and black, erupt in this superb flesh. The colors natural to life deepen, dance and disengage themselves around the Vision, in the making. And shudders rise and roar, and the frenzied flavor of these effects becoming laden with the mortal whistlings and the harsh music which the world, far behind us, flings at our mother of beauty, — she recoils, she draws herself up. Oh! our bones are invested with an amorous new body.

*

*　　*

O the ashen face, the shield of hair, the arms of crystal! the cannon on which I must swoop down through the clash of the trees and the buoyant air!

VII
Vies

I

O les énormes avenues du pays saint, les terrasses du temple! Qu'a-t-on fait du brahmane qui m'expliqua les Proverbes? D'alors, de là-bas, je vois encore même les vieilles! Je me souviens des heures d'argent et de soleil vers les fleuves, la main de la compagne sur mon épaule, et de nos caresses debout dans les plaines poivrées. — Un envol de pigeons écarlates tonne autour de ma pensée. — Exilé ici, j'ai eu une scène où jouer les chefs-d'œuvre dramatiques de toutes les littératures. Je vous indiquerais les richesses inouïes. J'observe l'histoire des trésors que vous trouvâtes. Je vois la suite! Ma sagesse est aussi dédaignée que le chaos. Qu'est mon néant, auprès de la stupeur qui vous attend?

II

Je suis un inventeur bien autrement méritant que tous ceux qui m'ont précédé; un musicien même, qui ai trouvé quelque chose comme la clef de l'amour. A présent, gentilhomme d'une campagne aigre au ciel sobre, j'essaye de m'émouvoir au souvenir de l'enfance mendiante, de l'apprentissage ou de l'arrivée en sabots, des polémiques, des cinq ou six veuvages, et quelques noces où ma forte tête m'empêcha de monter au diapason des camarades. Je ne regrette pas ma vieille part de gaieté divine: l'air sobre de cette aigre campagne alimente fort activement mon atroce scepticisme. Mais comme ce scepticisme ne peut désormais être mis en œuvre, et que d'ailleurs je suis dévoué à un trouble nouveau, — j'attends de devenir un très méchant fou.

VII
Lives

I

O the vast avenues of the Holy Land, the terraces of the temple! What has happened to the Brahman who explained Proverbs to me? From that time, from that place, I still see even the old women! I recall hours of silver and of sunlight near the rivers, the hand of my companion on my shoulder, and our caresses as we stood on the spice-scented plains. — A flight of scarlet pigeons thunders around my recollection. — Exiled here, I have had a stage on which to perform the dramatic masterworks of all literatures. I would point out to you unheard-of riches. I note the history of the treasures that you found. I see what follows! My wisdom is as much disdained as chaos. What is my nothingness, in comparison with the stupor that awaits you?

II

I am an inventor far more meritorious than all those who have preceded me; a musician too, who have found something like the key of love. At the present time, a gentleman of a harsh land with a sober sky, I try to be moved by the remembrance of my mendicant childhood, of my apprenticeship or of my arrival in wooden shoes, of my polemics, of my five or six widowerhoods, and of some drinking bouts at which my strong head kept me from rising to the pitch of my companions. I do not miss my old portion of divine gaiety: the sober air of this harsh countryside feeds quite actively my atrocious skepticism. But because this skepticism cannot hereafter be put to use, and since, furthermore, I am devoted to a new disturbance, — I expect to become a most malicious madman.

III

Dans un grenier où je fus enfermé à douze ans j'ai connu le monde, j'ai illustré la comédie humaine. Dans un cellier j'ai appris l'histoire. A quelque fête de nuit dans une cité du Nord j'ai rencontré toutes les femmes des anciens peintres. Dans un vieux passage à Paris on m'a enseigné les sciences classiques. Dans une magnifique demeure cernée par l'Orient entier j'ai accompli mon immense œuvre et passé mon illustre retraite. J'ai brassé mon sang. Mon devoir m'est remis. Il ne faut même plus songer à cela. Je suis réellement d'outre-tombe, et pas de commissions.

VIII
Départ

Assez vu. La vision s'est rencontrée à tous les airs.

Assez eu. Rumeurs des villes, le soir, et au soleil, et toujours.

Assez connu. Les arrêts de la vie. — O Rumeurs et Visions!

Départ dans l'affection et le bruit neufs!

IX
Royauté

Un beau matin, chez un peuple fort doux, un homme et une femme superbes criaient sur la place publique: « Mes amis, je veux qu'elle soit reine! » « Je veux être reine! » Elle riait et tremblait. Il parlait aux amis de révélation, d'épreuve terminée. Ils se pâmaient l'un contre l'autre.

En effet, ils furent rois toute une matinée, où les tentures carminées se relevèrent sur les maisons, et toute l'après-midi, où ils s'avancèrent du côté des jardins de palmes.

III

In a garret where I was locked up at the age of twelve I knew the world; I illustrated the human comedy. In a cellar I learned history. At some nighttime festival in a city of the North I met all the women of the early painters. In an old lane in Paris I was taught the classical sciences. In a magnificent residence surrounded by the entire Orient I completed my prodigious work and spent my illustrious retirement. I stirred up my blood. I am absolved of my duty. It must not even be considered anymore. I am really from beyond the grave, and without commitments.

VIII
Departure

Seen enough. The vision appeared in all atmospheres.

Had enough. Uproars of cities, in the evening, and in the sun, and always.

Known enough. The impasses of life. — O Uproars and Visions!

Departure into new affection and new clamor!

IX
Royalty

One fine morning, in the country of a very gentle people, a superb man and woman were crying out in the public square: "My friends, I want her to be queen!" "I want to be queen!" She laughed and trembled. He spoke to friends of revelation, of a trial terminated. They swooned against each other.

In fact, they were monarchs for an entire morning, during which crimson hangings were raised again on the houses, and for the entire afternoon, during which they moved forward toward the gardens of palm trees.

X
À une raison

Un coup de ton doigt sur le tambour décharge tous les sons et commence la nouvelle harmonie.

Un pas de toi, c'est la levée des nouveaux hommes et leur en-marche.

Ta tête se détourne: le nouvel amour! Ta tête se retourne, — le nouvel amour!

« Change nos lots, crible les fléaux, à commencer par le temps », te chantent ces enfants. « Élève n'importe où la substance de nos fortunes et de nos vœux », on t'en prie.

Arrivée de toujours, qui t'en iras partout.

XI
Matinée d'ivresse

O mon Bien! O mon Beau! Fanfare atroce où je ne trébuche point! Chevalet féerique! Hourra pour l'œuvre inouïe et pour le corps merveilleux, pour la première fois! Cela commença sous les rires des enfants, cela finira par eux. Ce poison va rester dans toutes nos veines même quand, la fanfare tournant, nous serons rendu à l'ancienne inharmonie. O maintenant nous si digne de ces tortures! rassemblons fervemment cette promesse surhumaine faite à notre corps et à notre âme créés: cette promesse, cette démence! L'élégance, la science, la violence! On nous a promis d'enterrer dans l'ombre l'arbre du bien et du mal, de déporter les honnêtetés tyranniques, afin que nous amenions notre très pur amour. Cela commença par quelques dégoûts et cela finit, — ne pouvant nous saisir sur-le-champ de cette éternité, — cela finit par une débandade de parfums.

X
To a Reason

One tap of your finger on the drum releases all sounds and begins the new harmony.

One step of yours, it's the levy of new men and their order to march.

Your head turns aside: the new love! Your head turns back, — the new love!

"Change our lots, destroy the plagues, beginning with time," these children chant to you. "Raise up, no matter where, the substance of our fortunes and of our desires," they beg you.

Having arrived from all times, you'll depart on all sides.

XI
Morning of Drunkenness

O *my* Good! O *my* Beautiful! Excruciating fanfare in which I do not stumble! Magical rack! Hurrah for the unheard-of work and for the marvelous body, for the first time! It began with the laughter of children, it will end with it. This poison will remain in all our veins even when, with the changing fanfare, we shall be surrendered to our former disharmony. O now let us, so deserving of these tortures! fervently summon up this superhuman promise made to our created body and soul: this promise, this madness! Elegance, knowledge, violence! We were promised that they would bury in darkness the tree of good and evil, that they would banish tyrannical proprieties, so that we might bring here our very pure love. It began with some repugnance, and it ends, — since we cannot at once grasp this eternity, — it ends with a stampede of perfumes.

Rire des enfants, discrétion des esclaves, austérité des vierges, horreur des figures et des objets d'ici, sacrés soyez-vous par le souvenir de cette veille. Cela commençait par toute la rustrerie, voici que cela finit par des anges de flamme et de glace.

Petite veille d'ivresse, sainte! quand ce ne serait que pour le masque dont tu nous as gratifié. Nous t'affirmons, méthode! Nous n'oublions pas que tu as glorifié hier chacun de nos âges. Nous avons foi au poison. Nous savons donner notre vie tout entière tous les jours.

Voici le temps des Assassins.

XII
Phrases

Quand le monde sera réduit en un seul bois noir pour nos quatre yeux étonnés, — en une plage pour deux enfants fidèles, — en une maison musicale pour notre claire sympathie, — je vous trouverai.

Qu'il n'y ait ici-bas qu'un vieillard seul, calme et beau, entouré d'un « luxe inouï », — et je suis à vos genoux.

Que j'aie réalisé tous vos souvenirs, — que je sois celle qui sait vous garrotter, — je vous étoufferai.

Quand nous sommes très-forts, — qui recule? très-gais, — qui tombe de ridicule? Quand nous sommes très-méchants, — que ferait-on de nous?

Parez-vous, dansez, riez. — Je ne pourrai jamais envoyer l'Amour par la fenêtre.

Ma camarade, mendiante, enfant monstre! comme ça t'est égal, ces malheureuses et ces manœuvres, et mes embarras.

Laughter of children, circumspection of slaves, austerity of virgins, horror of the countenances and objects of this place, may you be consecrated by the memory of this vigil. It began with all loutishness, behold that it ends with angels of fire and of ice.

Little vigil of drunkenness, sanctified! were it only for the mask you have conferred on us. We affirm you, method! We don't forget that yesterday you glorified each of our ages. We have faith in the poison. We know how to give up our entire life day after day.

This is the time of the Assassins.

XII
Phrases

When the world has been reduced to a single gloomy wood for our four astonished eyes, — to one beach for two faithful children, — to one musical house for our pure harmony, — I shall find you.

Let there be here on earth only a single old man, calm and beautiful, surrounded by an "unheard-of luxury," — and I am at your knees.

Let me have realized all your recollections, — let me be the girl who knows how to tie you up, — I shall choke you.

When we are most strong, — who recoils? most merry, — who collapses from ridicule? When we are most malicious, — what would they do with us?

Adorn yourself, dance, laugh. — I could never send Love out the window.

My comrade, beggar girl, monster child! how indifferent you are to these unfortunate women and these maneuvers, and my

Attache-toi à nous avec ta voix impossible, ta voix! unique flatteur de ce vil désespoir.

Une matinée couverte, en juillet. Un goût de cendres vole dans l'air; — une odeur de bois suant dans l'âtre, — les fleurs rouies, — le saccage des promenades, — la bruine des canaux par les champs, — pourquoi pas déjà les joujoux et l'encens?

J'ai tendu des cordes de clocher à clocher; des guirlandes de fenêtre à fenêtre; des chaînes d'or d'étoile à étoile, et je danse.

Le haut étang fume continuellement. Quelle sorcière va se dresser sur le couchant blanc? Quelles violettes frondaisons vont descendre!

Pendant que les fonds publics s'écoulent en fêtes de fraternité, il sonne une cloche de feu rose dans les nuages.

Avivant un agréable goût d'encre de Chine, une poudre noire pleut doucement sur ma veillée. — Je baisse les feux du lustre, je me jette sur le lit, et, tourné du côté de l'ombre, je vous vois, mes filles! mes reines!

XIII
Ouvriers

O cette chaude matinée de février! Le Sud inopportun vint relever nos souvenirs d'indigents absurdes, notre jeune misère.

Henrika avait une jupe de coton à carreau blanc et brun,

difficulties. Attach yourself to us with your impossible voice, your voice! unique flatterer of this vile despair.

An overcast morning, in July. A taste of ashes flies through the air; — a smell of wood sweating in the fireplace, — the retted flowers, — the devastation of the promenades, — the drizzle from the canals through the fields, — why not even now toys and incense?

I have stretched ropes from steeple to steeple; garlands from window to window; chains of gold from star to star, and I am dancing.

The high pond fumes continually. What sorceress is going to rise out of the white sunset? What violet foliage is going to fall!

While public funds are drained off in feasts of brotherhood, a bell of rose-colored fire is ringing in the clouds.

Reviving an agreeable savor of India ink, a black powder rains gently on my vigil. — I lower the lights of the chandelier, I throw myself on the bed, and, turned toward the darkness, I see you, my daughters! my queens!

XIII
Workers

O that warm morning in February! The unseasonable south wind came to revive our recollections of ridiculous paupers, our youthful misery.

Henrika had on a white and brown checked cotton skirt,

qui a dû être portée au siècle dernier, un bonnet à rubans et un foulard de soie. C'était bien plus triste qu'un deuil. Nous faisions un tour dans la banlieue. Le temps était couvert, et ce vent du Sud excitait toutes les vilaines odeurs des jardins ravagés et des prés desséchés.

Cela ne devait pas fatiguer ma femme au même point que moi. Dans une flache laissée par l'inondation du mois précédent à un sentier assez haut, elle me fit remarquer de très-petits poissons.

La ville, avec sa fumée et ses bruits de métiers, nous suivait très loin dans les chemins. O l'autre monde, l'habitation bénie par le ciel, et les ombrages! Le Sud me rappelait les misérables incidents de mon enfance, mes désespoirs d'été, l'horrible quantité de force et de science que le sort a toujours éloignée de moi. Non! nous ne passerons pas l'été dans cet avare pays où nous ne serons jamais que des orphelins fiancés. Je veux que ce bras durci ne traîne plus une *chère image*.

XIV
Les Ponts

Des ciels gris de cristal. Un bizarre dessin de ponts, ceux-ci droits, ceux-là bombés, d'autres descendant en obliquant en angles sur les premiers, et ces figures se renouvelant dans les autres circuits éclairés du canal, mais tous tellement longs et légers que les rives, chargées de dômes, s'abaissent et s'amoindrissent. Quelques-uns de ces ponts sont encore chargés de masures. D'autres soutiennent des mâts, des signaux, de frêles parapets. Des accords mineurs se croisent, et filent; des cordes montent des berges. On distingue une veste rouge, peut-être d'autres costumes et des instruments de musique. Sont-ce des airs populaires, des bouts de concerts seigneuriaux, des restants

which must have been worn in the last century, a bonnet with ribbons and a silk scarf. It was much sadder than a funeral procession. We were taking a walk in the suburbs. The weather was overcast, and that wind from the South stirred up all the vile odors of the ravaged gardens and the parched meadows.

It must not have fatigued my wife to the same degree as it did me. In a puddle left by the flood of the previous month on a rather high path, she called my attention to some very small fishes.

The city, with its smoke and its noises of trades, followed us very far along the roads. O the other world, the habitation blessed by the sky, and the shadows! The south wind reminded me of the miserable incidents of my childhood, my despairs in summer, the horrible amount of strength and of knowledge that fate has always kept away from me. No! we will not spend the summer in this miserly country where we'll never be anything but betrothed orphans. I wish that this hardened arm may no longer drag a *cherished image.*

XIV
The Bridges

Crystalline gray skies. A strange pattern of bridges, these straight, those arched, others descending obliquely at angles to the first, and these configurations repeating themselves in the other illuminated circuits of the canal, but all so long and light that the shores, laden with domes, sink and diminish. Some of these bridges are still encumbered with hovels. Others support masts, signals, frail parapets. Minor chords interweave, and flow smoothly; ropes rise from the steep banks. One detects a red jacket, perhaps other costumes and musical instruments. Are these popular tunes, fragments of manorial concerts, rem-

d'hymnes publics? L'eau est grise et bleue, large comme un bras de mer.

Un rayon blanc, tombant du haut du ciel, anéantit cette comédie.

XV
Ville

Je suis un éphémère et point trop mécontent citoyen d'une métropole crue moderne parce que tout goût connu a été éludé dans les ameublements et l'extérieur des maisons aussi bien que dans le plan de la ville. Ici vous ne signaleriez les traces d'aucun monument de superstition. La morale et la langue sont réduites à leur plus simple expression, enfin! Ces millions de gens qui n'ont pas besoin de se connaître amènent si pareillement l'éducation, le métier et la vieillesse, que ce cours de vie doit être plusieurs fois moins long que ce qu'une statistique folle trouve pour les peuples du continent. Aussi comme, de ma fenêtre, je vois des spectres nouveaux roulant à travers l'épaisse et éternelle fumée de charbon — notre ombre des bois, notre nuit d'été! — des Érinnyes nouvelles, devant mon cottage qui est ma patrie et tout mon cœur puisque tout ici ressemble à ceci, — la Mort sans pleurs, notre active fille et servante, un Amour désespéré et un joli Crime piaulant dans la boue de la rue.

XVI
Ornières

A droite l'aube d'été éveille les feuilles et les vapeurs et les bruits de ce coin du parc, et les talus de gauche tiennent dans leur ombre violette les mille rapides ornières de la route humide. Défilé de féeries. En effet: des chars chargés d'animaux

nants of public anthems? The water is gray and blue, ample as an arm of the sea.

A white ray, falling from the summit of the sky, reduces to nothingness this theatrical performance.

XV
City

I am a transitory and not too dissatisfied citizen of a metropolis deemed modern because all recognized taste has been avoided in the furnishings and the exterior of the houses as well as in the plan of the city. Here you would not mark the traces of a single monument to superstition. In short, morality and language are reduced to their simplest expression! These millions of people who have no need to know one another conduct their education, occupation and old age so similarly that their course of life must be several times shorter than that which an insane statistics establishes for the peoples of the continent. Also, as it were, from my window, I see new specters rolling through the thick and everlasting coal fumes — our forest shade, our summer night! — new Furies, in front of my cottage which is my homeland and all my heart since everything here looks like this, — Death without tears, our busy daughter and handmaiden, a Love despondent and a pretty Crime whining in the filth of the street.

XVI
Ruts

To the right the summer dawn wakens the leaves and the mists and the sounds of this corner of the park, and the banks on the left grip in their violet shade the thousand swift ruts of the wet road. Procession of enchantments. Quite so:

de bois doré, de mâts et de toiles bariolées, au grand galop de vingt chevaux de cirque tachetés, et les enfants et les hommes sur leurs bêtes les plus étonnantes; — vingt véhicules, bossés, pavoisés et fleuris comme des carrosses anciens ou de contes, pleins d'enfants attifés pour une pastorale suburbaine; — même des cercueils sous leur dais de nuit dressant les panaches d'ébène, filant au trot des grandes juments bleues et noires.

XVII
Villes

Ce sont des villes! C'est un peuple pour qui se sont montés ces Alleghanys et ces Libans de rêve! Des chalets de cristal et de bois qui se meuvent sur des rails et des poulies invisibles. Les vieux cratères ceints de colosses et de palmiers de cuivre rugissent mélodieusement dans les feux. Des fêtes amoureuses sonnent sur les canaux pendus derrière les chalets. La chasse des carillons crie dans les gorges. Des corporations de chanteurs géants accourent dans des vêtements et des oriflammes éclatants comme la lumière des cimes. Sur les plates-formes au milieu des gouffres les Rolands sonnent leur bravoure. Sur les passerelles de l'abîme et les toits des auberges l'ardeur du ciel pavoise les mâts. L'écroulement des apothéoses rejoint les champs des hauteurs où les centauresses séraphiques évoluent parmi les avalanches. Au-dessus du niveau des plus hautes crêtes, une mer troublée par la naissance éternelle de Vénus, chargée de flottes orphéoniques et de la rumeur des perles et des conques précieuses; — la mer s'assombrit parfois avec des éclats mortels. Sur les versants, des moissons de fleurs grandes comme nos armes et nos coupes, mugissent. Des cortèges de Mabs en robes rousses, opalines, montent des ravines. Là-haut, les pieds dans la cascade et les ronces, les cerfs tettent Diane.

chariots laden with animals of gilded wood, with masts and
multicolored sails, to the full gallop of twenty mottled circus
horses, both children and men on their most astonishing
beasts; — twenty vehicles, embossed, bedecked with flags and
adorned with flowers like ancient or storybook coaches, filled
with children costumed for a suburban pastoral; — even the
caskets under their canopy of night raising their ebony plumes,
filing past to the trot of the great blue-black mares.

XVII
Cities

What cities these are! This is a people for whom these dream
Alleghenies and Lebanons rose up! Chalets of crystal and
wood that move on invisible rails and pulleys. Old craters surrounded by colossi and copper palm trees roar melodiously in
the fires. Love feasts resound over canals suspended behind
chalets. The play of chimes clamors in the gorges. Guilds of
giant singers flock together with vestments and oriflammes as
dazzling as the light of the summits. On platforms in the midst
of whirlpools Rolands trumpet their bravery. On footbridges
of the abyss and roofs of the inns the fire of the sky adorns the
masts with flags. The collapse of apotheoses overtakes the
fields of the hilltops where seraphic centauresses revolve
among the avalanches. Above the level of the highest crests, a
sea troubled by the eternal birth of Venus, filled with choral
fleets and the murmur of precious pearls and conches; — the
sea grows somber sometimes with fatal flashes. On the slopes,
harvests of flowers large as our weapons and our goblets,
bellow. Processions of Mabs in russet robes, opaline, ascend
from the ravines. Up there, with their feet in the waterfall and
the brambles, deer nurse at Diana's breast. The Bacchantes

Les Bacchantes des banlieues sanglotent et la lune brûle et hurle. Vénus entre dans les cavernes des forgerons et des ermites. Des groupes de beffrois chantent les idées des peuples. Des châteaux bâtis en os sort la musique inconnue. Toutes les légendes évoluent et les élans se ruent dans les bourgs. Le paradis des orages s'effondre. Les sauvages dansent sans cesse la fête de la nuit. Et, une heure, je suis descendu dans le mouvement d'un boulevard de Bagdad où des compagnies ont chanté la joie du travail nouveau, sous une brise épaisse, circulant sans pouvoir éluder les fabuleux fantômes des monts où l'on a dû se retrouver.

Quels bons bras, quelle belle heure me rendront cette région d'où viennent mes sommeils et mes moindres mouvements?

XVIII
Vagabonds

Pitoyable frère! Que d'atroces veillées je lui dus! « Je ne me saisissais pas fervemment de cette entreprise. Je m'étais joué de son infirmité. Par mar faute nous retournerions en exil, en esclavage. » Il me supposait un guignon et une innocence très bizarres, et il ajoutait des raisons inquiétantes.

Je répondais en ricanant à ce satanique docteur, et finissais par gagner la fenêtre. Je créais, par delà la campagne traversée par des bandes de musique rare, les fantômes du futur luxe nocturne.

Après cette distraction vaguement hygiénique, je m'étendais sur une paillasse. Et, presque chaque nuit, aussitôt endormi, le pauvre frère se levait, la bouche pourrie, les yeux arrachés, — tel qu'il se rêvait! — et me tirait dans la salle en hurlant son songe de chagrin idiot.

of the suburbs sob and the moon burns and howls. Venus enters the caves of blacksmiths and of hermits. Groups of belfries sing the ideas of the peoples. From castles built of bone issues unknown music. All legends evolve and enthusiasms rush through the towns. The paradise of storms subsides. The savages dance ceaselessly in celebration of the night. And, once, I went down into the bustle of a boulevard of Bagdad where companies sang the joy of the new work, in a heavy breeze, going about unable to elude the fabulous phantoms of the mountains where one had to find himself again.

What good arms, what fine hour will give me back this region from which my slumbers and my slightest movements come?

XVIII
Vagabonds

Pitiable brother! What agonizing vigils I owed him! "I was not embracing this enterprise fervently. I had made sport of his infirmity. Through my fault we would return to exile, to slavery." He imagined me a very strange jinx and an innocence, and he supplied disquieting reasons.

I responded by snickering at this Satanic doctor, and finished by getting to the window. I created, beyond the countryside traversed by bands of rare music, phantoms of future nocturnal luxury.

After this vaguely hygienic diversion, I would stretch myself out on a straw mattress. And, almost every night, as soon as I was asleep, the poor brother would rise, his mouth decayed, his eyes torn out, — just as he saw himself in his dreams! — and while howling his illusion of idiotic grief, he'd drag me into the room.

J'avais en effet, en toute sincérité d'esprit, pris l'engagement de le rendre à son état primitif de fils du soleil, — et nous errions, nourris du vin des cavernes et du biscuit de la route, moi pressé de trouver le lieu et la formule.

XIX
Villes

L'acropole officielle outre les conceptions de la barbarie moderne les plus colossales. Impossible d'exprimer le jour mat produit par le ciel immuablement gris, l'éclat impérial des bâtisses, et la neige éternelle du sol. On a reproduit dans un goût d'énormité singulier toutes les merveilles classiques de l'architecture. J'assiste à des expositions de peinture dans des locaux vingt fois plus vastes qu'Hampton-Court. Quelle peinture! Un Nabuchodonosor norwégien a fait construire les escaliers des ministères; les subalternes que j'ai pu voir sont déjà plus fiers que des brahmanes, et j'ai tremblé à l'aspect des gardiens de colosses et officiers de constructions. Par le groupement des bâtiments, en squares, cours et terrasses fermées, on a évincé les cochers. Les parcs représentent la nature primitive travaillée par un art superbe. Le haut quartier a des parties inexplicables: un bras de mer, sans bateaux, roule sa nappe de grésil bleu entre des quais chargés de candélabres géants. Un pont court conduit à une poterne immédiatement sous le dôme de la Sainte-Chapelle. Ce dôme est une armature d'acier artistique de quinze mille pieds de diamètre environ.

Sur quelques points des passerelles de cuivre, des plates-formes, des escaliers qui contournent les halles et les piliers, j'ai cru pouvoir juger la profondeur de la ville! C'est le prodige dont je n'ai pu me rendre compte: quels sont les niveaux des

I had, in fact, in all sincerity of spirit, taken the pledge to restore him to his primitive state of son of the sun, — and we would wander, nourished by the wine of the caverns and the biscuit of the road, I hard pressed to find the place and the formula.

XIX
Cities

The official acropolis exceeds the most colossal conceptions of modern barbarity. Imposssible to convey the dull daylight produced by the immutably gray sky, the imperial splendor of the buildings, and the eternal snow on the ground. They have reproduced with a singular taste for enormity all the classical marvels of architecture. I attend exhibitions of painting in premises twenty times more vast than Hampton Court. What painting! A Norwegian Nebuchadnezzar had the staircases of the ministries built; the subordinates I was able to see are already prouder than Brahmans, and I trembled at the sight of the guardians of colossi and supervisors of structures. By the grouping of buildings, in squares, courtyards and enclosed terraces, they have ousted the coachmen. The parks exhibit primitive nature cultivated with a superb art. The upper quarter has some inexplicable parts: an arm of the sea, without boats, rolls its cover of blue sleet between quays laden with gigantic candelabra. A short bridge leads to a postern immediately beneath the dome of Sainte-Chapelle. This dome is an artistic framework of steel about fifteen thousand feet in diameter.

From some points of the copper footbridges, of the platforms, of the staircases which wind round the markets and the pillars, I thought I could judge the depth of the city! This is the marvel for which I was not able to account: what are the

autres quartiers sur ou sous l'acropole? Pour l'étranger de notre temps la reconnaissance est impossible. Le quartier commerçant est un circus d'un seul style, avec galeries à arcades. On ne voit pas de boutiques, mais la neige de la chaussée est écrasée; quelques nababs, aussi rares que les promeneurs d'un matin de dimanche à Londres, se dirigent vers une diligence de diamants. Quelques divans de velours rouge: on sert des boissons polaires dont le prix varie de huit cents à huit mille roupies. A l'idée de chercher des théâtres sur ce circus, je me réponds que les boutiques doivent contenir des drames assez sombres? Je pense qu'il y a une police; mais la loi doit être tellement étrange, que je renonce à me faire une idée des aventuriers d'ici.

Le faubourg, aussi élégant qu'une belle rue de Paris, est favorisé d'un air de lumière; l'élément démocratique compte quelques cents âmes. Là encore, les maisons ne se suivent pas; le faubourg se perd bizarrement dans la campagne, le « Comté » qui remplit l'occident éternel des forêts et des plantations prodigieuses où les gentilshommes sauvages chassent leurs chroniques sous la lumière qu'on a créée.

XX
Veillées

I

C'est le repos éclairé, ni fièvre ni langueur, sur le lit ou sur le pré.

C'est l'ami ni ardent ni faible. L'ami.

C'est l'aimée ni tourmentante ni tourmentée. L'aimée.

L'air et le monde point cherchés. La vie.

— Était-ce donc ceci?

— Et le rêve fraîchit.

levels of the other quarters above or below the acropolis? For the stranger of our time exploration is impossible. The business quarter is a circus in a single style, with galleries in arcades. One does not see any shops, but the snow of the roadway is trampled; a few nabobs, as rare as pedestrians on a Sunday morning in London, make their way towards a stagecoach of diamonds. A few divans of red velvet: polar drinks, whose price varies from eight hundred to eight thousand rupees, are served. At the thought of looking for theaters in this circus, I tell myself that the shops must contain some rather gloomy dramas? I think that there is a police force; but the law must be so strange, that I give up forming an idea of the adventurers of this place.

The suburb, as elegant as a beautiful street in Paris, is favored with an atmosphere of light; the democratic element comprises a few hundred souls. There, too, the houses do not follow each other; the suburb disappears strangely into the countryside, the "County" which fills the endless west with forests and with prodigious plantations where savage noblemen hunt their chronicles by the light which has been created.

XX
Vigils
I

It is repose illuminated, neither fever nor languor, on the bed or on the meadow.

It is the friend neither ardent nor feeble. The friend.

It is the loved one neither tormenting nor tormented. The loved one.

The air and the world unsought. Life.

— Was it this, then?

— And the dream grows cold.

II

L'éclairage revient à l'arbre de bâtisse. Des deux extrémités de la salle, décors quelconques, des élévations harmoniques se joignent. La muraille en face du veilleur est une succession psychologique de coupes de frises, de bandes atmosphériques et d'accidences géologiques. — Rêve intense et rapide de groupes sentimentaux avec des êtres de tous les caractères parmi toutes les apparences.

III

Les lampes et les tapis de la veillée font le bruit des vagues, la nuit, le long de la coque et autour du steerage.

La mer de la veillée, telle que les seins d'Amélie.

Les tapisseries, jusqu'à mi-hauteur, des taillis de dentelle teinte d'émeraude, où se jettent les tourterelles de la veillée.

. . . .

La plaque du foyer noir, de réels soleils des grèves: ah! puits des magies; seule vue d'aurore, cette fois.

XXI
Mystique

Sur la pente du talus, les anges tournent leurs robes de laine dans les herbages d'acier et d'émeraude.

Des prés de flammes bondissent jusqu'au sommet du mamelon. A gauche le terreau de l'arête est piétiné par tous les homicides et toutes les batailles, et tous les bruits désastreux filent leur courbe. Derrière l'arête de droite la ligne des orients, des progrès.

Et, tandis que la bande en haut du tableau est formée de la rumeur tournante et bondissante des conques des mers et des nuits humaines,

II

The lighting returns to the building shaft. From the two ends
of the hall, ordinary scenery, harmonic elevations conjoin. The
wall opposite the watcher is a psychological series of sections
of friezes, of atmospheric bands and of geological undulations.
— Intense and sudden dream of sentimental groups with beings
of all qualities among all semblances.

III

The lamps and the rugs of the vigil make the roar of waves,
at night, along the hull and around the steerage deck.

The sea of the vigil, like the breasts of Amélie.

The tapestries, halfway up, thickets of emerald-tinted lace,
into which the turtledoves of the vigil fling themselves.

. . . .

The slab of the black hearth, real suns of the shores: ah!
wells of magic; sole sight of dawn, this time.

XXI
Mystic

On the slope of the bank, angels fashion their robes of wool
in pastures of steel and of emerald.

Meadows of flames spring up to the summit of the knoll.
On the left the compost of the ridge is stamped down by all
the murderers and all the battles, and all the disastrous clamors
spin their curve. Behind the ridge at the right the path of
pearls, of progress.

And, while the band at the top of the picture is formed of
the twirling and rebounding murmur of the conches of seas
and of human nights,

La douceur fleurie des étoiles et du ciel et du reste descend en face du talus, comme un panier, — contre notre face, et fait l'abîme fleurant et bleu là-dessous.

XXII
Aube

J'ai embrassé l'aube d'été.

Rien ne bougeait encore au front des palais. L'eau était morte. Les camps d'ombres ne quittaient pas la route du bois. J'ai marché, réveillant les haleines vives et tièdes, et les pierreries regardèrent, et les ailes se levèrent sans bruit.

La première entreprise fut, dans le sentier déjà empli de frais et blêmes éclats, une fleur qui me dit son nom.

Je ris au wasserfall blond qui s'échevela à travers les sapins: à la cime argentée je reconnus la déesse.

Alors je levai un à un les voiles. Dans l'allée, en agitant les bras. Par la plaine, où je l'ai dénoncée au coq. A la grand'ville, elle fuyait parmi les clochers et les dômes, et, courant comme un mendiant sur les quais de marbre, je la chassais.

En haut de la route, près d'un bois de lauriers, je l'ai entourée avec ses voiles amassés, et j'ai senti un peu son immense corps. L'aube et l'enfant tombèrent au bas du bois.

Au réveil il était midi.

The flowery fragrance of the stars and of the sky and of the rest descends opposite the bank, like a basket, — against our face, and makes the abyss sweet-smelling and blue below.

XXII
Dawn

I embraced the summer dawn.

Nothing was stirring yet in front of the palaces. The water lay lifeless. Encamped shadows did not leave the woodland road. I stepped forth, arousing breaths alive and warm, and precious stones kept watch, and wings rose up without a sound.

My first enterprise was, in the path already filled with cool, pale glints, a flower that told me her name.

I laughed at the blond waterfall which tossed dishevelled hair across the pines: on the silvery summit I espied the goddess.

Then, one by one, I lifted her veils. In the lane, waving my arms. On the plain, where I gave the cock notice of her coming. In the city, she fled among the steeples and domes, and, running like a beggar across the marble quays, I pursued her.

On the upper part of the road, near a grove of laurels, I surrounded her with her massed veils, and I sensed somewhat her immeasurable body. Dawn and the child plunged to the bottom of the wood.

When I awoke, it was noon.

XXIII
Fleurs

D'un gradin d'or, — parmi les cordons de soie, les gazes grises, les velours verts et les disques de cristal qui noircissent comme du bronze au soleil, — je vois la digitale s'ouvrir sur un tapis de filigranes d'argent, d'yeux et de chevelures.

Des pièces d'or jaune semées sur l'agate, des piliers d'acajou supportant un dôme d'émeraudes, des bouquets de satin blanc et de fines verges de rubis entourent la rose d'eau.

Tels qu'un dieu aux énormes yeux bleus et aux formes de neige, la mer et le ciel attirent aux terrasses de marbre la foule des jeunes et fortes roses.

XXIV
Nocturne vulgaire

Un souffle ouvre des brèches opéradiques dans les cloisons, — brouille le pivotement des toits rongés, — disperse les limites des foyers, — éclipse les croisées.

Le long de la vigne, m'étant appuyé du pied à une gargouille, — je suis descendu dans ce carrosse dont l'époque est assez indiquée par les glaces convexes, les panneaux bombés et les sophas contournés. Corbillard de mon sommeil, isolé, maison de berger de ma niaiserie, le véhicule vire sur le gazon de la grande route effacée: et dans un défaut en haut de la glace de droite tournoient les blêmes figures lunaires, feuilles, seins.

— Un vert et un bleu très foncés envahissent l'image. Dételage aux environs d'une tache de gravier.

XXIII
Flowers

From a step of gold, — among cords of silk, gray gauzes, green velvets and crystal disks that darken like bronze in the sun, — I see the foxglove open on a carpet of silver filigree, of eyes and of hair.

Bits of yellow gold seeded in agate, pillars of mahogany supporting a dome of emeralds, bouquets of white satin and of fine rods of ruby surround the water rose.

Like a god with enormous blue eyes and configurations of snow, the sea and the sky attract to the marble terraces the multitude of young and hardy roses.

XXIV
Common Nocturne

One breath opens operatic fissures in the walls, — disturbs the pivoting of the rotting roofs, — dispels the boundaries of the hearths, — darkens the windows.

Along the vineyard, having rested with my foot on a gargoyle, — I stepped down into this carriage whose period is adequately indicated by the convex windows, bulging panels and contoured seats. Hearse of my slumber, isolated, shepherd's hut of my foolishness, the vehicle turns on the grass of the obliterated highway: and in a blemish at the top of the window on the right swirl pale lunar figures, leaves, breasts.

— A very deep green and blue invade the image. Unharnessing near a spot of gravel.

— Ici va-t-on siffler pour l'orage, et les Sodomes et les So-
lymes, et les bêtes féroces et les armées,
    (— Postillon et bêtes de songe reprendront-ils sous les plus
suffocantes futaies, pour m'enfoncer jusqu'aux yeux dans la
source de soie.)
    — Et nous envoyer, fouettés à travers les eaux clapotantes et
les boissons répandues, rouler sur l'aboi des dogues . . .
    — Un souffle disperse les limites du foyer.

XXV
Marine

Les chars d'argent et de cuivre —
Les proues d'acier et d'argent —
Battent l'écume, —
Soulèvent les souches des ronces.
Les courants de la lande,
Et les ornières immenses du reflux,
Filent circulairement vers l'est,
Vers les piliers de la forêt,
Vers les fûts de la jetée,
Dont l'angle est heurté par des tourbillons de lumière.

XXVI
Fête d'hiver

La cascade sonne derrière les huttes d'opéra-comique. Des
girandoles se prolongent, dans les vergers et les allées voisins
du méandre, — les verts et les rouges du couchant. Nymphes
d'Horace coiffées au Premier Empire. — Rondes Sibériennes,
Chinoises de Boucher.

— Here will one whistle for the tempest, and the Sodoms and the Solymas, and the wild beasts and the armies,

(— Will postilion and dream-animals return beneath the most suffocating forests, in order to sink me up to the eyes in the silken wellspring.)

— And send us, scourged through splashing waters and spilt drinks, to roll over the baying of the bulldogs . . .

— One breath dispels the boundaries of the hearth.

XXV
Seascape

Chariots of silver and of copper —
Prows of steel and of silver —
Beat the foam, —
Uproot the stubs of the briers.
The currents of the heath,
And the huge ruts of the reflux,
Veer in a circle toward the east,
Toward the pillars of the forest,
Toward the shafts of the pier,
Whose corner is struck by whirlwinds of light.

XXVI
Winter Festival

The waterfall resounds behind the sheds of the opéra-comique. The girandoles prolong, in the orchards and the lanes bordering the meandering stream, — the greens and the reds of the sunset. Horatian nymphs with hair dressed in the First Empire style. — Siberian roundelays, Chinese women by Boucher.

XXVII
Angoisse

Se peut-il qu'Elle me fasse pardonner les ambitions continuellement écrasées, — qu'une fin aisée répare les âges d'indigence,
— qu'un jour de succès nous endorme sur la honte de notre
inhabileté fatale?

(O palmes! diamant! — Amour! force! — plus haut que
toutes joies et gloires! — de toutes façons, partout, — Démon,
dieu, — jeunesse de cet être-ci: moi!)

Que les accidents de féerie scientifique et des mouvements
de fraternité sociale soient chéris comme restitution progressive de la franchise première? . . .

Mais la Vampire qui nous rend gentils commande que nous
nous amusions avec ce qu'elle nous laisse, ou qu'autrement
nous soyons plus drôles.

Rouler aux blessures, par l'air lassant et la mer; aux sup-
plices, par le silence des eaux et de l'air meurtriers; aux tortures
qui rient, dans leur silence atrocement houleux.

XXVIII
Métropolitain

Du détroit d'indigo aux mers d'Ossian, sur le sable rose et
orange qu'a lavé le ciel vineux viennent de monter et de se
croiser des boulevards de cristal habités incontinent par de
jeunes familles pauvres qui s'alimentent chez les fruitiers. Rien
de riche. — La ville!

Du désert de bitume fuient droit en déroute avec les nappes

XXVII
Anguish

Can it be that She will have me pardoned for ambitions perpetually shattered, — that an end in easy circumstances will
make amends for ages of indigence, — that one day of success
will lull us to sleep on the shame of our fatal incompetence?

(O palms! diamond! — Love! strength! — loftier than all
joys and glories! — of all modes, on all sides, — Demon, god, —
youth of this very being: myself!)

Can it be that the accidents of scientific magic and the
movements of social brotherhood will be cherished as the
progressive restitution of original freedom? . . .

But the Vampire who makes us gentle commands that we
amuse ourselves with what she permits us, or else be more
droll.

To toss on wounds, through the wearisome air and the sea;
on racks, through the silence of the murderous waters and air;
on tortures that laugh, in their cruelly swelling silence.

XXVIII
Metropolitan

From the indigo strait to the seas of Ossian, on the rose and
orange sand which the wine-colored sky has washed, crystal
boulevards have just risen and crossed, occupied immediately
by poor young families who get their food at the fruiterers'
shops. Nothing affluent. — The city!

From the asphalt desert there flee straight ahead in rout

de brumes échelonnées en bandes affreuses au ciel qui se re-
courbe, se recule et descend formé de la plus sinistre fumée
noire que puisse faire l'Océan en deuil, les casques, les roues,
les barques, les croupes. — La bataille!

Lève la tête: ce pont de bois, arqué; les derniers potagers
de Samarie; ces masques enluminés sous la lanterne fouettée
par la nuit froide; l'ondine niaise à la robe bruyante, au bas de
la rivière; les crânes lumineux dans les plants de pois, — et les
autres fantasmagories, — la campagne.

Des routes bordées de grilles et de murs, contenant à peine
leurs bosquets, et les atroces fleurs qu'on appellerait cœurs et
sœurs, Damas damnant de longueur, — possessions de fé-
eriques aristocraties ultra-Rhénanes, Japonaises, Guaranies,
propres encore à recevoir la musique des anciens, — et il y a des
auberges qui pour toujours n'ouvrent déjà plus; — il y a des
princesses, et, si tu n'es pas trop accablé, l'étude des astres, —
le ciel.

Le matin où, avec Elle, vous vous débattîtes parmi les éclats
de neige, les lèvres vertes, les glaces, les drapeaux noirs et les
rayons bleus, et les parfums pourpres du soleil des pôles, — ta
force.

XXIX
Barbare

Bien après les jours et les saisons, et les êtres et les pays,

Le pavillon en viande saignante sur la soie des mers et des
fleurs arctiques; (elles n'existent pas.)

Remis des vieilles fanfares d'héroïsme — qui nous attaquent
encore le cœur et la tête — loin des anciens assassins.

with sheets of fog echeloned in hideous bands on the sky that bends, recoils and sinks, formed of the most sinister black smoke which the Ocean in mourning can produce, helmets, wheels, barges, rumps. — The battle!

Raise your head: this wooden bridge, arched; the last truck gardens of Samaria; these maskers illuminated by the lantern lashed by the frigid night; the foolish water sprite in her noisy robe, at the bottom of the river; the luminous skulls among the pea seedlings, — and the other phantasmagories, — the countryside.

Roads bordered by railings and walls, scarcely restraining their thickets, and the dreadful flowers one might call hearts and sisters, Damascus damning with dullness, — possessions of fairy-tale aristocracies from beyond the Rhine, Japanese, Guaranian, still fit to receive the music of the ancients, — and there are some inns that now do not open anymore, and never will; — there are princesses, and, if you're not too overwhelmed, the study of the stars, — the sky.

The morning when, with Her, you struggled amid the spangles of snow, the green lips, the ice, the black flags and the azure rays, and the purple perfumes of the Polar sun, — your strength.

XXIX
Barbarian

Long after the days and the seasons, and the creatures and the countries,

The banner of bleeding meat on the silk of the seas and of the arctic flowers; (they do not exist.)

Delivered from the old fanfares of heroism — that still attack our heart and our head — far from the former assassins.

— Oh! le pavillon en viande saignante sur la soie des mers et des fleurs arctiques; (elles n'existent pas.)

Douceurs!

Les brasiers, pleuvant aux rafales de givre, — Douceurs! — les feux à la pluie du vent de diamants jetée par le cœur terrestre éternellement carbonisé pour nous. — O monde! —

(Loin des vieilles retraites et des vieilles flammes, qu'on entend, qu'on sent,)

Les brasiers et les écumes. La musique, virement des gouffres et choc des glaçons aux astres.

O Douceurs, ô monde, ô musique! Et là, les formes, les sueurs, les chevelures et les yeux, flottant. Et les larmes blanches, bouillantes, — ô douceurs! — et la voix féminine arrivée au fond des volcans et des grottes arctiques.

Le pavillon . . .

XXX
Promontoire

L'aube d'or et la soirée frissonnante trouvent notre brick en large en face de cette villa et de ses dépendances, qui forment un promontoire aussi étendu que l'Épire et le Péloponnèse ou que la grande île du Japon, ou que l'Arabie! Des fanums qu'éclaire la rentrée des théories; d'immenses vues de la défense des côtes modernes; des dunes illustrées de chaudes fleurs et de bacchanales; de grands canaux de Carthage et des embankments d'une Venise louche; de molles éruptions d'Etnas et des crevasses de fleurs et d'eaux des glaciers; des lavoirs entourés de peupliers d'Allemagne; des talus de parcs singuliers penchant des têtes d'Arbres du Japon; et les façades circulaires des « Royal » ou des « Grand » de Scarborough ou de Brook-

— Oh! the banner of bleeding meat on the silk of the seas and of the arctic flowers; (they do not exist.)

Delights!

Blazing coals, raining in squalls of hoarfrost, — Delights! — fires in the rain of the wind of diamonds, rain hurled down by the earthly heart eternally carbonized for us. — O world! —

(Far from the old retreats and the old flames, that are known, that are felt,)

Blazing coals and froths. Music, veering of whirlpools and collisions of drift ice with the stars.

O Delights, oh world, oh music! And there, the forms, the sweats, the heads of hair and the eyes, floating. And the white tears, boiling, — oh delights! — and the feminine voice borne down to the bottom of the volcanoes and the arctic grottoes.

The banner . . .

XXX
Promontory

Golden dawn and trembling evening find our brig at sea opposite this villa and its outbuildings, which form a promontory as extensive as Epirus and the Peloponnesus or as the great island of Japan, or as Arabia! The shrines which the reentry of the processions illuminates; vast vistas of the fortification of modern coasts; dunes decorated with blazing blooms and bacchanalia; grand canals of Carthage and embankments of a dubious Venice; feeble eruptions of Etnas and crevasses with flowers and the waters of glaciers; washhouses surrounded by German poplars; slopes of strange parks inclining the heads of Japanese trees; and the circular facades of the "Royal" or the "Grand" hotels of Scarborough or Brooklyn; and their railways

lyn; et leurs railways flanquent, creusent, surplombent les dispositions de cet hôtel, choisies dans l'histoire des plus élégantes et des plus colossales constructions de l'Italie, de l'Amérique et de l'Asie, dont les fenêtres et les terrasses, à présent pleines d'éclairages, de boissons et de brises riches, sont ouvertes à l'esprit des voyageurs et des nobles, — qui permettent, aux heures du jour, à toutes les tarentelles des côtes, — et même aux ritournelles des vallées illustres de l'art, de décorer merveilleusement les façades du Palais-Promontoire.

XXXI
Scènes

L'ancienne Comédie poursuit ses accords et divise ses idylles: Des boulevards de tréteaux.

Un long pier en bois d'un bout à l'autre d'un champ rocailleux ou la foule barbare évolue sous les arbres dépouillés.

Dans des corridors de gaze noire, suivant le pas des promeneurs aux lanternes et aux feuilles,

Des oiseaux comédiens s'abattent sur un ponton de maçonnerie mû par l'archipel couvert des embarcations des spectateurs.

Des scènes lyriques, accompagnées de flûte et de tambour, s'inclinent dans des réduits ménagés sur les plafonds autour des salons de clubs modernes ou des salles de l'Orient ancien.

La féerie manœuvre au sommet d'un amphithéâtre couronné de taillis, — ou s'agite et module pour les Béotiens, dans l'ombre des futaies mouvantes, sur l'arête des cultures.

L'opéra-comique se divise sur notre scène à l'arête d'intersection de dix cloisons dressées de la galerie aux feux.

flank, underlie, overhang the plans of this hotel, selected from the history of the most elegant and the most colossal structures of Italy, of America and of Asia, whose windows and terraces, at present full of costly lights, drinks and breezes, are open to the spirit of the travelers and the nobles, — who during daylight hours permit all the tarantellas of the coasts, — and also the ritornellos of the famed valleys of art, to decorate marvelously the facades of the Promontory-Palace.

XXXI
Scenes

Ancient Comedy pursues its harmonies and divides its idylls:
  Boulevards with stages.

A long wooden pier from one end to the other of a rocky field where the barbarous crowd moves around beneath the bare trees.

In corridors of black gauze, following the stride of the promenaders with lanterns and leaves,

Some performer birds swoop down upon a pontoon of masonry moved by the archipelago covered with the spectators' boats.

Lyrical scenes, accompanied by flute and drum, slope down into recesses arranged on the ceilings around the lounges of modern clubs or the halls of the ancient Orient.

The magic spectacle operates at the top of an amphitheater crowned with thickets, — or moves about and modulates for the Bocotians, in the shadow of the stirring forest trees, on the edge of the cultivated lands.

The opéra-comique is divided on our stage at the line of intersection of ten partitions erected between the gallery and the footlights.

XXXII
Soir historique

En quelque soir, par exemple, que se trouve le touriste naïf, retiré de nos horreurs économiques, la main d'un maître anime le clavecin des prés; on joue aux cartes au fond de l'étang, miroir évocateur des reines et des mignonnes; on a les saintes, les voiles, et les fils d'harmonie, et les chromatismes légendaires, sur le couchant.

Il frissonne au passage des chasses et des hordes. La comédie goutte sur les tréteaux de gazon. Et l'embarras des pauvres et des faibles sur ces plans stupides!

A sa vision esclave, l'Allemagne s'échafaude vers des lunes; les déserts tartares s'éclairent; les révoltes anciennes grouillent dans le centre du Céleste Empire; par les escaliers et les fauteuils de rocs un petit monde blême et plat, Afrique et Occidents, va s'édifier. Puis un ballet de mers et de nuits connues, une chimie sans valeur, et des mélodies impossibles.

La même magie bourgeoise à tous les points où la malle nous déposera! Le plus élémentaire physicien sent qu'il n'est plus possible de se soumettre à cette atmosphère personnelle, brume de remords physiques, dont la constatation est déjà une affliction.

Non! Le moment de l'étuve, des mers enlevées, des embrasements souterrains, de la planète emportée, et des exterminations conséquentes, certitudes si peu malignement indiquées dans la Bible et par les Nornes et qu'il sera donné à l'être sérieux de surveiller. — Cependant ce ne sera point un effet de légende!

XXXII
Historic Evening

On some evening, for example, when the naive tourist finds himself withdrawn from our economic horrors, the hand of a master animates the harpsichord of the meadows; people play cards at the bottom of the pond, mirror evocative of queens and favorites; there are saints, veils, and threads of harmony, and legendary chromatisms, in the sunset.

He shudders at the passing by of the hunts and the hordes. The play drips on the stage of sod. And the confusion of the poor and the weak over these stupid plots!

In his slavish vision, Germany raises herself on scaffolds toward the moons; the Tartar wildernesses light up; ancient revolts stir in the center of the Celestial Empire; on stairways and armchairs of rocks a little world, pale and flat, Africa and Western lands, is going to be built. Afterwards a ballet of well-known seas and nights, a worthless chemistry, and impossible melodies.

The same bourgeois magic at all points where the mail transport deposits us! The most elementary physicist feels that it is no longer possible to submit to this personal atmosphere, mist of physical remorse, whose ascertainment is already an affliction.

No! The moment of the sweating room, of the seas raised up, of the subterranean conflagrations, of the planet swept away, and of the ensuing exterminations, certainties indicated with so little malice in the Bible and by the Norns and which it will be granted to the serious person to inspect. — Nevertheless this will by no means be a result of legend!

XXXIII
Mouvement

Le mouvement de lacet sur la berge des chutes du fleuve,
Le gouffre à l'étambot,
La célérité de la rampe,
L'énorme passade du courant
Mènent par les lumières inouïes
Et la nouveauté chimique
Les voyageurs entourés des trombes du val
Et du strom.

Ce sont les conquérants du monde
Cherchant la fortune chimique personnelle;
Le sport et le confort voyagent avec eux;
Ils emmènent l'éducation
Des races, des classes et des bêtes, sur ce vaisseau
Repos et vertige
A la lumière diluvienne,
Aux terribles soirs d'étude.

Car de la causerie parmi les appareils, le sang, les fleurs,
   le feu, les bijoux,
Des comptes agités à ce bord fuyard,
— On voit, roulant comme une digue au delà de la
   route hydraulique motrice,
Monstrueux, s'éclairant sans fin, — leur stock d'études;
Eux chassés dans l'extase harmonique,
Et l'héroïsme de la découverte.

Aux accidents atmosphériques les plus surprenants,
Un couple de jeunesse s'isole sur l'arche,
      — Est-ce ancienne sauvagerie qu'on pardonne? —
Et chante et se poste.

XXXIII
Movement

The swaying movement on the steep bank of the river's falls,
The whirlpool at the sternpost,
The speed of the slope,
The enormous passing of the current
Conduct through the unheard-of lights
And the chemical innovation
The travelers surrounded by the waterspouts of the valley
And of the stream.

These are the conquerors of the world
Seeking their personal chemical fortune;
Sport and comfort travel with them;
They take away the education
Of races, of classes and of animals, on this ship
Repose and vertigo
In the diluvial light,
In terrible nights of study.

For from the talk amid the apparatus, the blood, the flowers,
    the fire, the jewels,
From the agitated accounts aboard this fugitive ship,
— One sees, rolling like a dike beyond the hydraulic power
    road,
Monstrous, lighting up endlessly, — their stock of studies;
The people driven into harmonic ecstasy,
And the heroism of discovery.

In the most amazing atmospheric accidents,
A youthful couple isolates itself on the ark,
        — Is it primitive savagery that people pardon? —
And sings and takes its post.

XXXIV
Bottom

La réalité étant trop épineuse pour mon grand caractère, — je me trouvai néanmoins chez ma dame, en gros oiseau gris-bleu s'essorant vers les moulures du plafond et traînant l'aile dans les ombres de la soirée.

Je fus, au pied du baldaquin supportant ses bijoux adorés et ses chefs-d'œuvre physiques, un gros ours aux gencives violettes et au poil chenu de chagrin, les yeux aux cristaux et aux argents des consoles.

Tout se fit ombre et aquarium ardent.

Au matin, — aube de juin batailleuse, — je courus aux champs, âne, claironnant et brandissant mon grief, jusqu'à ce que les Sabines de la banlieue vinrent se jeter à mon poitrail.

XXXV
H

Toutes les monstruosités violent les gestes atroces d'Hortense. Sa solitude est la mécanique érotique; sa lassitude, la dynamique amoureuse. Sous la surveillance d'une enfance, elle a été, à des époques nombreuses, l'ardente hygiène des races. Sa porte est ouverte à la misère. Là, la moralité des êtres actuels se décorpore en sa passion ou en son action. — O terrible frisson des amours novices sur le sol sanglant et par l'hydrogène clarteux! trouvez Hortense.

XXXIV
Bottom

Reality being too thorny for my noble nature, — I found myself nevertheless at my lady's house, as a large blue-gray bird soaring toward the moldings of the ceiling and dragging my wing in the shadows of the evening.

I was, at the foot of the baldachin supporting her adored jewels and her physical masterpieces, a big bear with violet gums and fur gray with grief, my eyes on the cut glass and the silverware of the consoles.

Everything became shadow and glowing aquarium.

In the morning, — combative June dawn, — I ran to the fields, an ass, trumpeting and brandishing my grievance, until the Sabines of the suburbs came to fling themselves on my breast.

XXXV
H

All the monstrosities violate the atrocious behavior patterns of Hortense. Her solitude is erotic mechanics; her lassitude, amorous dynamics. Under the supervision of childhood, she has been, in numerous epochs, the ardent hygiene of races. Her door is open to misery. There, the morality of actual beings is disembodied in her passion or in her action. — O terrible thrill of new loves on the bloodstained soil and through the transparent hydrogen! find Hortense.

XXXVI
Dévotion

A ma sœur Louise Vanaen de Voringhem: — Sa cornette bleue tournée à la mer du Nord. — Pour les naufragés.

A ma sœur Léonie Aubois d'Ashby. Baou! — l'herbe d'été bourdonnante et puante. — Pour la fièvre des mères et des enfants.

A Lulu, — démon — qui a conservé un goût pour les oratoires du temps des Amies et de son éducation incomplète. Pour les hommes. — A madame***.

A l'adolescent que je fus. A ce saint vieillard, ermitage ou mission.

A l'esprit des pauvres. Et à un très haut clergé.

Aussi bien à tout culte en telle place de culte mémoriale et parmi tels événements qu'il faille se rendre, suivant les aspirations du moment ou bien notre propre vice sérieux.

Ce soir, à Circeto des hautes glaces, grasse comme le poisson, et enluminée comme les dix mois de la nuit rouge — (son cœur ambre et spunk), — pour ma seule prière muette comme ces régions de nuit et précédant des bravoures plus violentes que ce chaos polaire.

A tout prix et avec tous les airs, même dans des voyages métaphysiques. — Mais plus *alors*.

XXXVI
Devotion

To my sister Louise Vanaen de Voringhem: — Her blue coif turned toward the North Sea. — For the shipwrecked.

To my sister Léonie Aubois d'Ashby. Baou! — the summer's grass buzzing and stinking. — For the fever of mothers and of children.

To Lulu, — demon — who has retained a taste for the chapels of the time of the *Amies* and of her incomplete education. For the men. — To Madame * * *.

To the adolescent that I was. To this saintly old man, hermitage or mission.

To the spirit of the poor. And to a very high clergy.

Moreover, to every cult in such place of memorial cult and among such occurrences that it may be necessary to surrender, following the aspirations of the moment or else our own serious vice.

This evening, to Circeto of the towering ice, fat as the fish, and flushed like the ten months of the red night — (her heart amber and spunk), — for my only prayer silent like these regions of night and preceding acts of bravery more violent than this polar chaos.

At any price and in all atmospheres, even in metaphysical travels. — But no more *after that*.

XXXVII
Démocratie

« Le drapeau va au paysage immonde, et notre patois étouffe le tambour.

« Aux centres nous alimenterons la plus cynique prostitution. Nous massacrerons les révoltes logiques.

« Aux pays poivrés et détrempés! — au service des plus monstrueuses exploitations industrielles ou militaires.

« Au revoir ici, n'importe où. Conscrits du bon vouloir, nous aurons la philosophie féroce; ignorants pour la science, roués pour le confort; la crevaison pour le monde qui va. C'est la vraie marche. En avant, route! »

XXXVIII
Fairy

Pour Hélène se conjurèrent les sèves ornementales dans les ombres vierges et les clartés impassibles dans le silence astral. L'ardeur de l'été fut confiée à des oiseaux muets et l'indolence requise à une barque de deuils sans prix par des anses d'amours morts et de parfums affaissés.

Après le moment de l'air des bûcheronnes à la rumeur du torrent sous la ruine des bois, de la sonnerie des bestiaux à l'écho des vals, et des cris des steppes.

Pour l'enfance d'Hélène frissonnèrent les fourrés et les ombres, et le sein des pauvres, et les légendes du ciel.

Et ses yeux et sa danse supérieurs encore aux éclats précieux, aux influences froides, au plaisir du décor et de l'heure uniques.

XXXVII
Democracy

"The flag fits the foul landscape, and our dialect stifles the drum.

"In the centers we shall support the most cynical prostitution. We shall destroy the logical revolts.

"To the spicy and sodden lands! — at the service of the most monstrous industrial or military exploitations.

"Till we meet again here, no matter where. Conscripts of good will, we shall have our ferocious philosophy; ignorant as regards science, crafty for comfort; let the rest of the world drop dead. That's real progress. Forward, let's go!"

XXXVIII
Fairy

For Hélène the ornamental saps conspired in the virgin shadows and the impassive lights in the stellar silence. Summer's ardor was entrusted to the songless birds and the indolence proper to a priceless mourning barge through coves of dead loves and weakened perfumes.

After the interval of the song by the woodcutters' wives to the clamor of the torrent below the ruin of the woods, of the ringing of the cattle bells to the echo of the valleys, and of the cries of the steppes.

For Hélène's childhood, thickets and shadows shivered, and the bosoms of the poor, and the legends of heaven.

And her eyes and her dancing, superior even to precious sparkles, to cold influences, to the delight of the unique setting and hour.

XXXIX
Guerre

Enfant, certains ciels ont affiné mon optique: tous les caractères nuancèrent ma physionomie. Les phénomènes s'émurent. A présent, l'inflexion éternelle des moments et l'infini des mathématiques me chassent par ce monde où je subis tous les succès civils, respecté de l'enfance étrange et des affections énormes. Je songe à une guerre, de droit ou de force, de logique bien imprévue.

C'est aussi simple qu'une phrase musicale.

XL
Génie

Il est l'affection et le présent puisqu'il a fait la maison ouverte à l'hiver écumeux et à la rumeur de l'été, lui qui a purifié les boissons et les aliments, lui qui est le charme des lieux fuyants et le délice surhumain des stations. Il est l'affection et l'avenir, la force et l'amour que nous, debout dans les rages et les ennuis, nous voyons passer dans le ciel de tempête et les drapeaux d'extase.

Il est l'amour, mesure parfaite et réinventée, raison merveilleuse et imprévue, et l'éternité: machine aimée des qualités fatales. Nous avons tous eu l'épouvante de sa concession et de la nôtre: ô jouissance de notre santé, élan de nos facultés, affection égoïste et passion pour lui, lui qui nous aime pour sa vie infinie . . .

Et nous nous le rappelons et il voyage . . . Et si l'Adoration s'en va, sonne, sa promesse sonne: « Arrière ces supersti-

XXXIX
War

When I was a child, certain skies refined my vision: all their aspects shaded my countenance. Phenomena were roused. At present, the eternal modulation of moments and the infinity of mathematics pursue me through this world where, respected by strange children and by enormous affections, I meet with all civil successes. I dream of a war, of right or of force, of logic quite unforeseen.

It is as simple as a musical phrase.

XL
Genie

He is affection and the present since he has made the house open to frothy winter and to the hum of summer, he who has purified drink and food, he who is the charm of transitory places and the superhuman delight of stopping places. He is affection and the future, strength and love which we, standing within our rages and ennuis, see passing in the stormy sky and the flags of ecstasy.

He is love, perfect and reinvented measure, marvelous and unforeseen reason, and eternity: beloved engine of fatal qualities. We have all experienced the terror of his concession and of ours: oh rapture of our health, transport of our faculties, egotistical affection and passion for him, for him who loves us for his unending life . . .

And we recall him and he travels . . . And if the Adoration goes away, rings, his promise rings: "Away with these super

tions, ces anciens corps, ces ménages et ces âges. C'est cette époque-ci qui a sombré! »

Il ne s'en ira pas, il ne redescendra pas d'un ciel, il n'accomplira pas la rédemption des colères de femmes et des gaietés des hommes et de tout ce péché: car c'est fait, lui étant, et étant aimé.

O ses souffles, ses têtes, ses courses: la terrible célérité de la perfection des formes et de l'action!

O fécondité de l'esprit et immensité de l'univers!

Son corps! le dégagement rêvé, le brisement de la grâce croisée de violence nouvelle!

Sa vue, sa vue! tous les agenouillages anciens et les peines *relevés* à sa suite.

Son jour! l'abolition de toutes souffrances sonores et mouvantes dans la musique plus intense.

Son pas! les migrations plus énormes que les anciennes invasions.

O Lui et nous! l'orgueil plus bienveillant que les charités perdues.

O monde! et le chant clair des malheurs nouveaux!

Il nous a connus tous et nous a tous aimés. Sachons, cette nuit d'hiver, de cap en cap, du pôle tumultueux au château, de la foule à la plage, de regards en regards, forces et sentiments las, le héler et le voir, et le renvoyer, et, sous les marées et au haut des déserts de neige, suivre ses vues, ses souffles, son corps, son jour.

stitions, these ancient bodies, these households and these ages. It is this epoch which has foundered!"

He will not go away, he will not redescend from a heaven, he will not accomplish the redemption of women's rages and of men's gaieties and of all this sin: for it is done, because of his being, and being loved.

O his breaths, his brains, his journeys: the astounding swiftness of the perfection of forms and of action!

O fecundity of the spirit and immensity of the universe!

His body! the dreamed-of deliverance, the shattering of grace met with new violence!

His presence, his presence! all the ancient genuflections and the penalties *released* in his wake.

His day! the abolition of all resonant and moving sufferings in more intense music.

His step! migrations more enormous than the ancient invasions.

O He and we! the pride more benevolent than the lost charities.

O world! and the clear song of new misfortunes!

He has known us all and has loved us all. May we know, this winter night, from cape to cape, from the tumultuous pole to the castle, from the crowd to the beach, from glances to glances, strengths and tired feelings, how to hail him and to see him, and to send him away, and, under the tides and to the top of the wastelands of snow, to follow his ideas, his breaths, his body, his day.

XLI
Jeunesse

I

DIMANCHE

Les calculs de côté, l'inévitable descente du ciel et la visite des souvenirs et la séance des rhythmes occupent la demeure, la tête et le monde de l'esprit.

— Un cheval détale sur le turf suburbain et le long des cultures et des boisements, percé par la peste carbonique. Une misérable femme de drame, quelque part dans le monde, soupire après des abandons improbables. Les desperadoes languissent après l'orage, l'ivresse et les blessures. De petits enfants étouffent des malédictions le long des rivières.

Reprenons l'étude au bruit de l'œuvre dévorante qui se rassemble et remonte dans les masses.

II

SONNET

Homme de constitution ordinaire, la chair n'était-elle pas un fruit pendu dans le verger, ô journées enfantes! le corps un trésor à prodiguer; ô aimer, le péril ou la force de Psyché? La terre avait des versants fertiles en princes et en artistes, et la descendance et la race nous poussaient aux crimes et aux deuils: le monde, votre fortune et votre péril. Mais à présent, ce labeur comblé, toi, tes calculs, toi, tes impatiences ne sont plus que votre danse et votre voix, non fixées et point forcées, quoique d'un double événement d'invention et de succès une raison, en l'humanité fraternelle et

XLI
Youth

I
SUNDAY

When calculations are put aside, the inevitable descent from heaven and the visit of memories and the performance of rhythms occupy the home, the head and the world of the spirit.

— A horse, riddled with carbonic plague, takes off on the suburban turf and along the cultivated fields and the woodlands. A miserable woman from a drama, somewhere in the world, sighs for improbable surrenders. Desperadoes long for tumult, drunkenness and wounds. Little children stifle curses along the rivers.

Let us resume our study to the din of the consuming work which gathers and rises again among the masses.

II
SONNET

Man of average constitution, was not the flesh a fruit suspended in the orchard, O childish days! the body a treasure to squander; O to love, the peril or the power of Psyche? The earth had slopes teeming with princes and artists, and descent and race drove us to crimes and to sorrows: the world, your fortune and your peril. But now, with that labor completed, you, your calculations, you, your fits of impatience are no more than your dancing and your voice, not fixed and not at all forced, although a reason for a double outcome of invention and success, in fraternal and con-

discrète par l'univers sans images; — la force et le droit réfléchissent la danse et la voix à présent seulement appréciées . . .

III
VINGT ANS

Les voix instructives exilées . . . L'ingénuité physique amèrement rassise . . . Adagio. Ah! l'égoïsme infini de l'adolescence, l'optimisme studieux: que le monde était plein de fleurs cet été! Les airs et les formes mourant . . . Un chœur, pour calmer l'impuissance et l'absence! Un chœur de verres de mélodies nocturnes . . . En effet les nerfs vont vite chasser.

IV

Tu en es encore à la tentation d'Antoine. L'ébat du zèle écourté, les tics d'orgueil puéril, l'affaiblissement et l'effroi. Mais tu te mettras à ce travail: toutes les possibilités harmoniques et architecturales s'émouvront autour de ton siège. Des êtres parfaits, imprévus, s'offriront à tes expériences. Dans tes environs affluera rêveusement la curiosité d'anciennes foules et de luxes oisifs. Ta mémoire et tes sens ne seront que la nourriture de ton impulsion créatrice. Quant au monde, quand tu sortiras, que sera-t-il devenu? En tout cas, rien des apparences actuelles.

XLII
Solde

A vendre ce que les Juifs n'ont pas vendu, ce que noblesse ni crime n'ont goûté, ce qu'ignore l'amour maudit et la probité infernale des masses; ce que le temps ni la science n'ont pas à reconnaître:

siderate humanity in the universe devoid of images;
— might and right reflect the dancing and the voice,
only now appreciated . . .

III

AGE TWENTY

Instructive voices banished . . . Physical ingenuousness bitterly appeased . . . Adagio. Ah! the infinite egoism of adolescence, the studious optimism: how full of flowers the world was that summer! The airs and the forms dying . . . A choir, to soothe impotence and absence! A choir of glasses of nocturnal melodies . . . Indeed, the nerves are quickly going to hunt.

IV

You're still subject to the temptation of Anthony. The frolic of diminished zeal, the twitches of puerile pride, the depression and the dread. But you'll devote yourself to this work: all harmonic and architectural possibilities will rise about your seat. Perfect beings, unforeseen, will offer themselves for your experiments. About you will flow dreamily the curiosity of ancient crowds and of idle luxuries. Your memory and your senses will be but the nourishment of your creative impulse. As for the world, when you depart, what will it have become? At any rate, nothing like present appearances.

XLII
Clearance Sale

For sale what the Jews have not sold, what neither nobility nor crime has tasted, what accursed love and the infernal probity of the people do not know; what neither time nor science has to acknowledge:

Les Voix reconstituées; l'éveil fraternel de toutes les énergies chorales et orchestrales et leurs applications instantanées; l'occasion, unique, de dégager nos sens!

A vendre les corps sans prix, hors de toute race, de tout monde, de tout sexe, de toute descendance! Les richesses jaillissant à chaque démarche! Solde de diamants sans contrôle!

A vendre l'anarchie pour les masses; la satisfaction irrépressible pour les amateurs supérieurs; la mort atroce pour les fidèles et les amants!

A vendre les habitations et les migrations, sports, féeries et conforts parfaits, et le bruit, le mouvement et l'avenir qu'ils font!

A vendre les applications de calcul et les sauts d'harmonie inouïs. Les trouvailles et les termes non soupçonnés, possession immédiate.

Élan insensé et infini aux splendeurs invisibles, aux délices insensibles, et ses secrets affolants pour chaque vice et sa gaîté effrayante pour la foule.

A vendre les corps, les voix, l'immense opulence inquestionable, ce qu'on ne vendra jamais. Les vendeurs ne sont pas à bout de solde! Les voyageurs n'ont pas à rendre leur commission de sitôt!

The Voices restored; the fraternal awakening of all choral and orchestral energies and their instantaneous applications; the opportunity, unique, to free our senses!

For sale priceless bodies, beyond any race, any world, any sex, any lineage! Riches springing up at every step! Clearance sale of diamonds without control!

For sale anarchy for the masses; irrepressible satisfaction for superior amateurs; excruciating death for the faithful and the lovers!

For sale settlements and migrations, sports, fairylands and perfect comforts, and the noise, the movement and the future they create!

For sale applications of calculation and unprecedented leaps of harmony. Discoveries and terms not suspected, immediate possession.

Mad and endless transport to invisible splendors, to unconscious delights, and its bewildering secrets for every vice and its grim gaiety for the crowd.

For sale the bodies, the voices, the immense, unquestionable opulence, that which will never be sold. The vendors have not reached the end of their clearance sale! The travelers will not have to render their commission for some time to come!

Index of French Titles

Index of English Titles